Multi-Agency Public Protection Arrangements and Youth Justice

Edited by Kerry Baker and Alex Sutherland

First published in Great Britain in 2009 by The Policy Press

The Policy Press
University of Bristol
Fourth Floor, Beacon House
Queen's Road
Bristol BS8 1QU
UK

Tel no +44 (0)117 331 4054
Fax no +44 (0)117 331 4093
E-mail tpp-info@bristol.ac.uk
www.policypress.org.uk

North American office:
The Policy Press
c/o International Specialized Books Services
920 NE 58th Avenue, Suite 300
Portland, OR 97213-3786, USA
tel +1 503 287 3093, fax +1 503 280 8832
e-mail info@isbs.com

© The Policy Press 2009

ISBN 978 1 84742 215 6

British Library Cataloguing in Publication Data
A catalogue record for this report is available from the British Library.

Library of Congress Cataloging-in-Publication Data
A catalog record for this report has been requested.

Cover image courtesy of iStockphoto®
Cover design by Qube Design Associates, Bristol
Printed in Great Britain by Latimer Trend, Plymouth

Contents

Acknowledgements

This book has developed from a study and symposium both funded by the Youth Justice Board (YJB) for England and Wales and we would like to thank the YJB for its generous support in these endeavours.

We are grateful to the research participants who gave up their time for the original study and whose ideas and thoughts drove a lot of the debate and subsequent work. We are indebted to the presenters and participants at the symposium for their views and engagement with the issue of Multi-Agency Public Protection Arrangements (MAPPA) and youth justice. Our thanks also go to Gill Kelly, Bernadette Wilkinson and David Goode for their helpful comments. Finally, we would like to thank our co-contributors for the time and effort they have given to this work.

Kerry Baker and Alex Sutherland

Notes on contributors

Kerry Baker is a researcher at the Centre for Criminology at the University of Oxford and also a consultant to the Youth Justice Board (YJB) on issues of assessment, risk and public protection. She has been closely involved in the development and validation of the *Asset* assessment tool currently used by all Youth Offending Teams (YOTs) in England and Wales. She has experience of working with both practitioners and policy makers in this field and has developed guidance for youth justice staff on a range of public protection issues.

Sarah Jones worked at the Centre for Criminology at the University of Oxford between 2000 and 2007, completing various research and evaluation projects. One of these projects was an investigation of the use of MAPPA for young people. Sarah is currently the Research Manager at Revolving Doors Agency in London – a research and development charity dedicated to the needs of people who are caught in a cycle of crisis, crime and mental illness.

Hazel Kemshall is currently Professor of Community and Criminal Justice at De Montfort University. Her research interests include the assessment and management of high-risk offenders, Multi-Agency Public Protection Panels and community responses to sexual offenders. She has written extensively on risk, public protection and dangerousness, and has completed research for the Home Office, Scottish Executive and the Economic and Social Research Council.

Fergus McNeill is Professor of Criminology and Social Work at the Glasgow School of Social Work and at the Scottish Centre for Crime and Justice Research, University of Glasgow. Prior to becoming an academic in 1998, Fergus worked for a number of years in residential drug rehabilitation and as a criminal justice social worker. His research interests have addressed a range of criminal justice issues including sentencing, community penalties and youth justice. Latterly his work has focused on the policy and practice implications of research evidence about the process of desistance from offending.

David Monk is Head of Practice Framework and Innovation at the YJB for England and Wales and was previously London Regional Manager for the YJB. Before that, he worked for the London Probation Area and as Assistant Chief Probation Officer in the late 1990s held policy and strategic responsibility for the probation service's work with sex offenders. His current responsibilities at the YJB include (among others) oversight of developments in relation to assessment, public protection, safeguarding and serious incidents involving children and young people in community and secure settings.

Alex Sutherland is currently studying for a doctorate in sociology at the University of Oxford. His thesis explores the application of explanatory theories of crime to adolescent substance use. He was a researcher at the Centre for Criminology at the University of Oxford between 2001 and 2007. During this time he worked on a number of projects, notably the evaluation of Intensive Supervision and Surveillance Programmes and a recent collaboration with Sarah Jones on MAPPA in youth justice.

Noel Whitty is Professor of Human Rights Law at the University of Nottingham. His current research is centred on prisoner and ex-offender governance within the UK, focusing in particular on the relationship between risk assessment, risk management practices and human rights law.

Jason Wood is a senior lecturer in youth and community development at De Montfort University with a particular interest in the community management of high-risk offenders. In 2006, he led a study into the operation and experience of MAPPA as part of the Child Sex Offender Review commissioned by the Home Secretary. Together with Hazel Kemshall, he has published numerous chapters and articles on risk, public protection and the development of MAPPA.

Introduction

Alex Sutherland and Kerry Baker

> Public protection, particularly of children and the most vulnerable, is this Government's priority. (David Blunkett, cited in Home Office, 2002, p 5)

> The way we deal with those who break the law is fundamental to the health of our society. (Charles Clarke, cited in Home Office, 2006, p 5)

Framing the debate

Public protection is always high on the political agenda in one form or another. The phrase 'public protection' began life within the criminal justice sphere as part of the government White Paper *Crime, Justice and Protecting the Public* (Home Office, 1990, cited in Merrington and Stanley, 2007, p 437). Since its introduction into the political lexicon, 'public protection' has been transformed into an umbrella term to cover a range of activities by local authorities and other government agencies,[1] but within the context of this book the phrase relates solely to serious offending (that is, violent and sexual offences). Although the phrase may have been formally introduced fairly recently, '[t]he probation service has been accountable for the protection of the public from serious offending ever since it took responsibility for the supervision of released prisoners in the 1960s' (Merrington and Stanley, 2007, p 437). A long-running topic within the criminal justice literature has been what the state's response should be to those individuals who threaten serious harm to others (see Bottoms, 1977). Current debates in criminology focus on security and the governance of criminal justice (Zedner, 2003; Loader and Walker, 2007). Multi-Agency Public Protection Arrangements (MAPPA), as their name suggests, are a part of this debate. Until now, much of the discussion about MAPPA has focused on their application to adults. More recently, however, there has been a growing academic and political interest in the use of MAPPA for young people. The ways in which organisations, charged with the task of managing the risks posed by young people, view and treat those they are working with is a critical nexus where conflicting assumptions about 'being young' are laid bare, and where the difficulties encountered by criminal justice agencies in working with the young are most apparent. The contributions included in this book offer insights into these issues from a range of perspectives and highlight a number of areas, both practical and theoretical, that require further attention.

A (brief) history of risk

There is an extensive literature devoted to the 'rise of risk' across a range of subjects, and it will not be repeated here.[2] There are, however, some relevant key points arising from this literature that serve as useful terms of reference before delving further into this book.

The first important point from this literature is that the concept of risk has moved from being something that is 'unknowable' to that which appears 'predictable'. Lupton (1999) points out that the hazards of plague, war and famine were more prevalent for past generations than they are now. However, at the time, these events were seen as natural and essentially outside of human control – for example as an act of God (Ewald, 1993). The progression from risk as an unknowable externality to something calculable has been attributed to a wide range of factors (see Kemshall et al, 1997; Lupton, 1999; Rigakos and Hadden, 2001). The important point is that increasingly the mathematical and scientific approaches to risk supplanted previous ideas for explaining human behaviour. In the midst of this, Castell (1991, p 281) argues that the 'scientific' approach led away from the idea of 'a subject or concrete individual' to one where the person is atomised into 'a combination of factors, the factors of risk. Thus, if we understand risk to be 'the effect of a combination of abstract factors' (1991, p 287) affecting the likelihood of an undesirable behaviour occurring, this, it is argued, makes human behaviour more susceptible to analysis and prediction.

A second point of interest is the (re)conceptualisation of risk as a negative. The modernist understanding of risk presents it as a morally neutral term, relating only to the probability of an event occurring. However, the 20th century has seen a transferral of this meaning away from neutral probability to negative danger. As Douglas makes clear makes clear '[t]he word *risk* now means danger; *high risk* means lots of danger' (1992, p 24; emphasis in original).

Finally, we should be conscious of the fact that perceptions of those who present a risk to society change over time. In the early 19th century, for example, the greatest threats to social order and stability came from 'dangerous classes' rather than dangerous individuals (Pratt, 2000). From the mid-19th century onwards, this shifted towards individuals who were seen as presenting a risk to society; for example repeat property offenders (Pratt, 1997) and, latterly, violent and sexual offenders (Nash, 1992). Bottoms (1977) highlighted the selective way that risk categories are applied, an issue that has also been highlighted again more recently by Tombs and Whyte (2008). Since 11 September 2001, we have seen a recategorisation of those who present the 'real risk' to the principles of (Western) society to include terrorists and religious extremists. There is also an increasing concern about those engaged in 'single issue' protests (such as animal rights, anti-war, anti-globalisation and anti-genetically modified crops).[3]

Government and the governance of risk

Concerns about risk – and subsequent strategies employed to control it – have a long history (see Lupton, 1999). Despite the fact that there are competing ideas about the conceptualisation of risk (Brown, 2000; Kemshall, 2002), the shift towards apparent predictability and the location of risk within individuals rather than groups or 'classes' means that the 'probabilistic discourse is still prevalent in much government policy' (Kemshall, 2002, p 15). While, as O'Malley (1992) argues, there may be an increasing expectation that individuals and communities should protect themselves from crime, the idea that the state has a duty to protect its citizens is still widely accepted. This is based primarily on the fact that it is difficult to insure against events (such as crime or flooding), which are relatively rare, hard to predict and that can lead to large, even irredeemable losses. As a result, citizens still demand that the apparatus of the state provides protection against these kinds of risks.

The forms of control employed to minimise risks posed by offenders have been many and varied throughout the course of history; from the magic and superstition of premodern societies, the prevalence of corporal punishments through much of history, right through to the technologically dependent surveillance methods of the late-modern age. Within this, there have been numerous debates and legislative drives focused on what to do with those who present a threat of serious harm to others. Through various manifestations, the control of this small group of individuals has tended to focus on a lengthy prison sentence in one form or another (primarily on an incapacitative basis; see Ashworth, 2007; Levi et al, 2007). The proliferation of criminal justice legislation as a means by which government can control the risks posed by offenders was paralleled by an emphasis on risk assessment and the implementation of risk management procedures for offenders being released from prison, or otherwise supervised in the community. A paradigmatic example of this drive for controlling risk forms the primary subject matter for this book.

MAPPA

MAPPA are discussed at length in this volume and, consequently, the introduction to them here will be brief. In essence, MAPPA are a mechanism by which agencies can work together in managing the risks presented by those who present a high risk of harm to others and/or whose actions have drawn high levels of attention from the public and the media. MAPPA are a relatively new phenomenon, beginning in 2001 and initially aimed at adult sex offenders. Over time, this remit has expanded to include violent offenders and other 'high-profile' cases. MAPPA are about risk management, not risk elimination: at their most simple they are a set of arrangements and a forum for multi-agency cooperation. Their dual purpose is to ensure that relevant information about an individual is shared between those agencies who have responsibility for managing the potential for violent and/or sexual offending by specific individuals; and where required, to access services and resources that enable practitioners to manage this risk. This book gives an overview of the complexities for practitioners and policy makers that arise from trying to manage, in the community, individuals who present a risk of serious harm to others.

With some notable exceptions (see Kemshall and colleagues, cited throughout this volume), MAPPA have not been the focus of extensive research. What research there has been has looked mainly at the form and function of MAPPA for adults. The operation of MAPPA and Youth Offending Teams (YOTs) has come under limited scrutiny from Her Majesty's Inspectorate for Probation (HMIP) but detail in this area has been meagre. Its annual report on YOTs in England and Wales (HMIP, 2007) was the first to explicitly mention MAPPA, stating that 'improvements have been seen in the involvement of YOTs into [MAPPA]' (2007, p 25) and that there was 'good integration' into these arrangements (2007, p 29).

The Oxford MAPPA study and symposium

Recognising the paucity of knowledge around the operation of MAPPA with young people, the Youth Justice Board (YJB) commissioned research in 2007 to explicitly study the engagement of YOTs with MAPPA. The resulting study (Sutherland and Jones, 2008) found that, in some instances, YOTs were entirely disengaged from the MAPPA process and that problems with identifying eligible cases were common.

The interest encountered by Sutherland and Jones while conducting their research led to a symposium on the subject, also funded by the YJB, which took place on 12 December 2007 at Nuffield College, Oxford. The purpose of the symposium was to bring together academics, practitioners and policy makers to discuss a range of research findings and discuss their views on the management of young people who present a risk of serious harm to others. Five papers were presented, which are reflected in some of the chapters of this book with the addition of two more contributions that substantially add to the debate.

Chapter summaries

The book is divided into two parts. Part One (Chapters One to Four) is concerned primarily with the current state of community risk management in England and Wales, highlighting previous research in this area and setting out future directions for investigation. Part Two (Chapters Five to Seven) widens this debate with contributions that introduce ideas about risk management from Scotland, examine the form and function of discretion in the current system and seek to reframe the debate on MAPPA and young people in terms of rights and risks.

In opening Part One, Sarah Jones and Kerry Baker (Chapter One) outline key features of the youth justice system in England and Wales, including the current focus on risk assessment and targeted interventions. In doing this, they set out some of the multiple responsibilities that YOTs have towards young people and the various partnerships that they are expected to engage with. In setting the scene, the reader is provided with a basic overview of MAPPA. The chapter concludes by highlighting critical questions raised by the intersection of risk, rights and welfare in youth justice.

In Chapter Two, Hazel Kemshall and Jason Wood consider what might be learnt from previous experience in the adult system of how MAPPA operate. Rather than suggest that the adult approach is what is required, they put forward a strong case for the differential treatment of young people within this context, suggesting that adults' interpretation of risky decisions by young people as 'irrational' should be tempered with knowledge about how young people perceive risks and the context within which risky behaviour takes place. In addition, the conceptualisation of young people as risk takers should be balanced with knowledge about possible protective factors that may ameliorate these risks.

In Chapter Three, Alex Sutherland focuses on the practical issues facing YOTs when they engage with MAPPA. First, he gives a summary of the research that this chapter is based on. He then identifies a number of possible difficulties that stem from both a historical lack of cooperation between YOTs and MAPPA, and recent changes in the focus of youth justice. Further, Sutherland invites the reader to think about the impact that local adult offender populations might have on the decision-making process at MAPPA meetings. In concluding, he argues that YOT inclusion in MAPPA should mean a wider engagement in this area with YOT agendas and responsibilities, not a whole-hearted adoption of MAPPA priorities.

There can be no question that policy making in this area is fraught with difficulties. Concluding Part One, David Monk (Chapter Four) highlights key principles that underpin the development of public protection within youth justice in England and Wales. In addition, some of the developments stemming from key partnerships (for instance between the YJB and the Parole Board) are also detailed. Finally, the impact of forthcoming revisions to National Standards and the implementation of a risk-based approach to practice are discussed, with the emphasis that good policy will come from good partnerships.

Bearing in mind the lessons learnt from England and Wales, Fergus McNeill (Chapter Five) reflects on the introduction of public protection arrangements for adults (defined as those aged 16+) in Scotland. Despite a number of similarities between the two systems, particularly in the concerns raised about the introduction of a system that is quasi-legal, McNeill notes a preference for different modes of intervention north of the border. Primarily, he notes that strengths-based initiatives (such as the Good Lives Model) may offer more scope for rehabilitation and reintegration than the risk-needs-responsivity approach that currently dominates much of public protection policy.

In Chapter Six, Kerry Baker draws our attention to the use of discretion within MAPPA. She notes that discretion is able to peep through the cracks of public protection and that in some places can be widely exercised by those operating on the front line of practice. While this discretion can be exercised, it is bounded within what she (borrowing from Dworkin, 1978) terms the prescriptive MAPPA 'doughnut'. Baker argues that the conceptualisation of risk also has implications in this area, specifically that risk aversion (based on 'othering') may lead to exclusionary practices, but on the other hand, risk-based practice can potentially encompass more inclusive and rehabilitative approaches if staff have the appropriate skills to exercise professional discretion in their choice of interventions.

In Chapter Seven, as a stark example of the difficulties that policy makers will face in the future as MAPPA develop within youth justice (and elsewhere), Noel Whitty outlines the tension and interplay between governance, risk and human rights. He challenges the idea that the choice facing criminal justice (and other state agencies) is risk or rights; pointing out that the reality is a negotiated landscape of risk and rights where organisations are faced with dual requirements to comply with both. Locating this debate within the specific example of MAPPA and youth justice, he wonders 'Is MAPPA for kids?' and queries the extent to which this question has been debated. Furthermore, he argues that criminal justice agencies must not forego more complex considerations about rights when faced with the vagaries of risk and the near dominant mantra of public protection.

In the concluding chapter, Kerry Baker and Alex Sutherland bring together the central themes of the book and raise a number of questions about the ways in which young people are treated by criminal justice agencies, and whether MAPPA as currently conceptualised are an appropriate system for effectively working with young people who have committed serious offences. They also highlight areas where further information is required and demonstrate that the study of MAPPA is a fertile ground for furthering debates around risk and rights. Finally, they suggest that lessons can be learnt from the implementation of MAPPA in Scotland and Northern Ireland, which can usefully inform the ongoing development of youth justice policy in England and Wales.

Notes

[1] Some examples include food hygiene standards, noise levels, pest control, dog ownership and the licensing of outdoor events (see, for example, the listing under the Public Protection Division, Cheltenham Borough Council: www.cheltenham.gov.uk).

[2] Those interested in the criminal justice angle might first consult Kemshall (2003), who extensively references risk in other fields.

[3] These are examples of what has been termed 'domestic extremism' in the latest version of the MAPPA guidance (Ministry of Justice, 2007, section 13).

References

Ashworth, A. (2007) 'Sentencing', in M. Maguire, R. Morgan and R. Reiner (eds) *The Oxford Handbook of Criminology* (4th edition, pp 990-1023), Oxford: Oxford University Press.

Bottoms, A. (1977) 'Reflections on the renaissance of dangerousness', *Howard Journal*, vol 16, no 2, pp 70-96.

Brown, M. (2000) 'Calculations of risk in contemporary penal practice', in M. Brown and J. Pratt (eds) *Dangerous Offenders: Punishment and Social Order*, London: Routledge.

Castell, D. (1991) 'From dangerousness to risk', in G. Burchell, C. Gordon and P. Miller (eds) *The Foucault Effect: Studies in Governmentality*, London: Harvester/ Wheatsheaf.

Douglas, M. (1992) *Risk and Blame: Essays in Cultural Theory*, London: Routledge.

Dworkin, R. (1978) *Taking Rights Seriously*, London: Duckworth.

Ewald, F. (1993) 'Two infinities of risk', in B. Massumi (ed) *The Politics of Everyday Fear*, Minneapolis, MN: University of Minnesota Press.

HMIP (Her Majesty's Inspectorate of Probation) (2007) *Joint Inspection of Youth Offending Teams Annual Report 2006/2007*, London: HMIP.

Home Office (2002) *Protecting the Public: Strengthening Protection Against Sex Offenders and Reforming the Law on Sexual Offences*, London: The Stationery Office.

Home Office (2006) *A Five Year Strategy for Protecting the Public and Reducing Re-offending*, London: The Stationery Office.

Kemshall, H. (2002) *Risk Assessment and Management of Serious Violent and Sexual Offenders: A Review of Current Issues*, Edinburgh: Scottish Executive.

Kemshall, H. (2003) *Understanding Risk in Criminal Justice*, Buckingham: Open University Press.

Kemshall, H., Parton, N., Walsh, M. and Waterson, J. (1997) 'Concepts of risk in relation to organizational structure and functioning within the personal social services and Probation', *Social Policy & Administration*, vol 31, no 3, pp 213-32.

Levi, M., Maguire, M. and Brookman, F. (2007) 'Violent crime', in M. Maguire, R. Morgan and R. Reiner (eds) *The Oxford Handbook of Criminology* (4th edition, pp 687-732), Oxford: Oxford University Press.

Loader, I. and Walker, N. (2007) *Civilizing Security*, Cambridge: Cambridge University Press.

Lupton, D. (1999) *Risk*, London: Routledge.

Merrington, S. and Stanley, S. (2007) 'Effectiveness: who counts what?', in L. Gelsthorpe and R. Morgan (eds) *Handbook of Probation* (pp 428-58), Cullompton: Willan.

Ministry of Justice (2007) *MAPPA Guidance Version 2.0*, National Offender Management Service, London: Ministry of Justice.

Nash, M. (1992) 'Dangerousness revisited', *International Journal of the Sociology of Law*, vol 20, no 4, pp 337-49.

O'Malley, P. (1992) 'Risk, power and crime prevention', *Economy and Society*, vol 21, no 3, pp 252-75.

Pratt, J. (1997) *Governing the Dangerous: Dangerousness, Law and Social Change*, Sydney: Federation Press.

Pratt, J. (2000) 'Dangerousness and modern society', in M. Brown and J. Pratt (eds) *Dangerous Offenders: Punishment and Social Order*, London: Routledge.

Rigakos, G.S. and Hadden, R.W. (2001) 'Crime, capitalism and the "risk society": towards the same olde modernity?', *Theoretical Criminology*, vol 5, no 1, pp 61-84.

Sutherland, A. and Jones, S. (2008) *MAPPA and Youth Justice: An Exploration of Youth Offending Team Engagement with Multi-Agency Public Protection Arrangements*, London: Youth Justice Board.

Tombs, S. and Whyte, D. (2008) *A Crisis of Enforcement: The Decriminalisation of Death and Injury at Work*, London: Centre for Crime and Justice Studies.

Zedner, L. (2003) 'Too much security?', *International Journal of the Sociology of Law*, vol 31, no 3, pp 155-84.

Part One
Young people and MAPPA: current policy and practice

Setting the scene: risk, welfare and rights

Sarah Jones and Kerry Baker

Introduction

This chapter will provide a brief introduction to systems for responding to offending by children and young people in England and Wales, of which Multi-Agency Public Protection Arrangements (MAPPA) are one significant element. The aims of the chapter are to:

- provide an overview of the youth justice system in England and Wales for readers who may be unfamiliar with it;
- explain what MAPPA are and how they work;
- begin to highlight some of the complexities of the system as a foundation for the more detailed analysis and discussion of later chapters.

MAPPA, as described in more detail below, are a set of arrangements for monitoring and managing offenders who have been assessed as presenting a high risk of serious harm to others. To understand the current operation of MAPPA with regard to young people, it is necessary to consider this quite specific practice issue within the wider context of recent developments in youth justice, which in turn reflect political and public concerns about serious offending by young people. The chapter therefore begins with an outline of the current youth justice system before moving on to a discussion of some of the questions raised by the introduction of MAPPA.

The youth justice system in England and Wales

More detailed histories of the development of the juvenile justice – now youth justice – system are available elsewhere (Bottoms and Dignan, 2004; Morgan and Newburn, 2007). The aim here is simply to provide an overview of the current framework and procedures for dealing with children and young people who offend. Although the origins of the youth justice system can be traced back over a century or more, major reforms were introduced by the 1998 Crime and Disorder Act, leading to what some have described as the 'new youth justice' (Goldson, 2000).

Structure and governance

Section 37 of the 1998 Crime and Disorder Act stated that '[i]t shall be the principal aim of the youth justice system to prevent offending by children and young people' and all those who work within youth justice are required to have regard to that statutory aim. Other significant reforms introduced by the Act were the introduction of the Youth Justice Board for England and Wales (YJB) as a non-departmental public body with responsibility for monitoring the operation of the youth justice system, advising ministers, the dissemination of research and (from 2000) the commissioning of places from the secure estate for young people receiving custodial sentences.

The Act also introduced new multi-agency Youth Offending Teams (YOTs) which bring together professionals from a range of disciplines.[1] Statutory involvement is required from local authority social services and education departments (now children's services), the police, probation service and health authorities. Other agencies, such as housing or youth and community departments, and specialist services around substance misuse or mental health, also work in partnership with YOTs.

Youth justice is not a national service; each YOT is accountable to the local authority in its area. The role of the YJB includes setting the framework for practice, for example through National Standards (YJB, 2004a), and providing guidance for YOTs on a range of topics, including MAPPA (YJB, 2006). Although there is greater structure and conformity in the system than previously, it is still the responsibility of local teams to decide on exactly how services for young people who offend should be organised and delivered.

Other key features of the reformed system include an emphasis on:

* early intervention;
* multi-agency working and partnership;
* risk assessment, identification and targeting of services;
* promotion of public and sentencer confidence;
* community participation and lay involvement.

There has been much debate about the impact of these reforms, with many arguing that they represent a shift towards a more punitive and risk-based way of working, which neglects the needs of often troubled young people (Pitts, 2001; Goldson and Muncie, 2006; Solomon and Garside, 2008). Others have suggested a more complex reality with measures such as the increased focus on restorative justice being implemented alongside some of the more punitive approaches, with the end result being that the system is now 'somewhat tricky to characterize' (Newburn, 2002, p 559). More recently, developments such as the emergence of Children's Trusts (YJB, 2004b) and changes to local performance frameworks[2] are having an impact on the way YOTs operate and further changes are likely in the light of recent government policy announcements (DCSF and Ministry of Justice, 2008).

Sentences and orders

The age of criminal responsibility in England and Wales is 10 years and young people between the ages of 10 and 17 are dealt with either by a youth court or, for more serious cases, by the Crown Court. There are currently a number of community sentences available (NACRO, 2006), although most will be replaced by the new Youth Rehabilitation Order (YRO), which will be introduced as a result of the 2008 Criminal Justice and Immigration Act. Custodial sentences available to courts include the Detention and Training Order (DTO) or, for more serious offences, young people can be sentenced under Sections 90/91 of the 2000 Powers of Criminal Courts (Sentencing) Act. The 2003 Criminal Justice Act also introduced two new 'public protection sentences' – the indeterminate sentence of 'detention for public protection' (Section 226) and the determinate 'extended sentence' (Section 228), which can be imposed where a court assesses a young person as being 'dangerous' (Sentencing Guidelines Council, 2008).

Recent legislation has attempted to clarify the purpose of sentencing in regard to young people. The 2008 Criminal Justice and Immigration Act states that courts must have regard to the principal aim of the youth justice system, which is to prevent offending and reoffending (Section 9(2)(a)). Courts must also have regard to the welfare of the offender in accordance with Section 44 of the 1933 Children and Young Person's Act and in addition should take account of the following factors (Section 9(3)):

- the punishment of offenders;
- the reform and rehabilitation of offenders;
- the protection of the public;
- the making of reparation by offenders to persons affected by their offences.

This sentencing gallimaufry is similar to that set out for adult offenders by the 2003 Criminal Justice Act, which has been criticised for the way that tensions between the different aims are ignored (Ashworth, 2007). Rather than providing clarification, therefore, it is possible that the 2008 Act could instead add to the confusion over the purpose of sentencing for young people (Baker, 2008). Any significant changes to sentencing patterns could affect the number of young people who become eligible for MAPPA although at the time of writing it is too early to say what the impact of the Act will be.

Assessment and interventions

Comprehensive assessment is seen by the YJB as an essential foundation for effective work with young people who offend (YJB, 2008a). One of the first acts of the newly established YJB was to commission the development of a standard risk assessment tool for use in all YOTs. This reflected parallel developments at that time in the probation service and social services towards the use of standardised assessment frameworks (Kemshall et al, 1997; Merrington, 2004). The assessment framework, known as *Asset*, has a number of different purposes. For example, it is designed to:

- help practitioners assess three key areas or types of risk: the likelihood of reoffending, the risk of serious harm occurring to others and the risk of the young person being harmed (termed 'vulnerability');
- prompt assessment of a wide range of risk and protective factors associated with offending by young people;
- produce a score indicative of the likelihood of reoffending;
- measure change over time;
- trigger further specialist assessments where needed (for example in relation to substance misuse, mental health or literacy).

Asset comprises a suite of materials with the central element being the core *Asset* profile, which is completed on all young people at the Pre-Sentence Report stage to inform the proposals that YOTs make to courts. Of particular relevance to MAPPA is the additional Risk of Serious Harm form (ROSH), which is triggered in cases where the core *Asset* indicates that there may be a likelihood of a young person causing serious harm to others. The ROSH form produces a risk classification, which will be a significant factor in decisions made by YOTs regarding the referral of young people to MAPPA. In addition to *Asset*, YOTs may use a range of other specialist assessment tools, for example in relation to young people who sexually abuse or young people with mental health needs.

The assessment should form the basis for planned interventions with a young person that are individually tailored according to the likelihood of reoffending and the specific risk and protective factors identified (YJB, 2008a). As multi-agency organisations, YOTs should be able to either directly provide or facilitate access to a wide range of services for young people to address the underlying factors contributing to their offending behaviour. The minimum frequency of contact between a YOT and a young person and requirements in relation to breach and enforcement are set out in National Standards (YJB, 2004a). The content of interventions is a matter for individual practitioners, although the YJB expects YOTs to have regard to its Key Elements of Effective Practice (KEEPs), which aim to set out research-based evidence on key features of effective service provision. Increasing attention is also now being given again to the importance of high-quality relationships between workers and young people (YJB, 2008b).

Safeguarding/welfare

As noted earlier, courts must have regard to Section 44 of the 1933 Children and Young Person's Act and there are a number of other statutory provisions relating to the welfare of young people that apply to the youth justice system. The 1989 Children Act set out a comprehensive framework with regard to local authorities' responsibilities for young people 'in need' (Sections 17 and 47 have particular relevance) and subsequent legal decisions have confirmed that these measures apply to young people in custody. In particular, the 'Munby judgment'[3] established that, where required, children in custody should be assessed under the Act to ascertain either their current needs or their needs on release back into the community. This has proved to be a difficult and contentious issue, with some local authorities reluctant to assess a young person's future needs on release[4] but the courts have reaffirmed the importance of such assessments for children leaving custody (Hollingsworth, 2007).

The 2004 Children Act states that YOTs are one of the statutory partners of the children's services authority and 'must co-operate with the authority in the making of arrangements' as required to improve 'the well-being of children' (Sections 10 and 25 for England and Wales respectively). Sections 11 and 28 (for England and Wales respectively) impose a duty on such partners to ensure that services and statutory responsibilities 'are discharged having regard to the need to safeguard and promote the welfare of children' (HM Government, 2007). The Act also established Local Safeguarding Children Boards (LSCBs), which bring together representatives from a range of agencies to coordinate and ensure the effectiveness of any work undertaken for the purpose of promoting and safeguarding the welfare of children in that area. Youth Offending Teams and governors of prisons or secure training centres are among those who should be represented on LSCBs (HM Government, 2006).

The extent to which the youth justice system should address young people's welfare needs remains a subject of ongoing debate, both in relation to the underlying principles of practice (Bottoms and Kemp, 2007) and with regard to specific points of decision making such as the parole process (Hollingsworth, 2007).

Protecting and promoting children's rights

Issues of children's rights are now receiving increasing attention in this area, particularly with regard to how instruments such as the United Nations Convention on the Rights of the Child (UNCRC), which was adopted in 1989 and ratified by the UK government in 1991, and the United Nations Standard Minimum Rules for the Administration of Juvenile Justice (the 'Beijing rules') should affect youth justice systems and practice.

Interestingly, this is an area where there appears to be a divergence in policy between England and Wales with, for example, the Welsh Assembly Government 'Seven Core Aims for Children and Young People' being more explicitly linked to the UNCRC than the equivalent 'Every Child Matters' programme in England. For example, the Children's Commissioner for England has stated his view about youth justice as follows: 'the system is not overtly UNCRC compliant in contrast to other countries I visited' (Aynsley-Green, 2007). Organisations such as the Howard League and the Children's Rights Alliance for England are increasingly focusing attention on rights for young people in contact with the criminal justice system and this is an issue likely to have an increasing impact on practice (see Whitty, this volume, for a more detailed discussion).

MAPPA

A relatively small number of children and young people will, during the course of their contact with the youth justice system, be referred to local MAPPA. These are the statutory arrangements for managing violent and sexual offenders. MAPPA are not a statutory body but 'a mechanism through which agencies can better discharge their statutory responsibilities and protect the public in a coordinated manner' (Ministry of Justice, 2007, p 8).

Purpose and organisation of MAPPA

MAPPA were formally created by Sections 67 and 68 of the 2000 Criminal Justice and Court Services Act, although they had evolved from multi-agency arrangements in the late 1990s for the assessment and management of sex offenders. These arrangements were consolidated by the 2003 Criminal Justice Act, which made the police, the probation service and prisons 'Responsible Authorities' while also placing a 'duty to cooperate' on other agencies. This legislation places a statutory responsibility on the three main agencies as follows:

- to establish arrangements for assessing and managing the risks posed by sexual and violent offenders;
- to review and monitor the arrangements;
- as part of the reviewing and monitoring arrangements, to prepare and publish an annual report on their operation.

Section 325 of the 2003 Criminal Justice Act specifies the agencies that have a duty to cooperate with MAPPA; these include Jobcentre Plus, the local education authority; local housing authorities and, significantly for this chapter, YOTs. The MAPPA guidance (Ministry of Justice, 2007) defines the purpose of involving such agencies as:

- to coordinate the involvement of different agencies in accessing and managing risk;
- to enable every agency, which has a legitimate interest, to contribute as fully as its existing statutory role and functions requires in a way that complements the work of other agencies.

The question of whether YOTs are appropriately designated as 'duty to cooperate' agencies or whether, given their role in the direct day-to-day management of offenders, they should become one of the Responsible Authority partners is a subject of ongoing debate (see Sutherland; and Monk, this volume).

The Strategic Management Board (SMB) in each area oversees and monitors the operation of MAPPA and should be comprised of senior representatives of each of the Responsible Authority and 'duty to cooperate' agencies. There should also be two lay members on each SMB who assist in reviewing how MAPPA work: 'their value is as informed observers and as posers of questions which the professionals closely involved in the work might not necessarily think of asking' (Ministry of Justice, 2007, p 114).

Identification, risk assessment and risk management

There are three categories of offenders eligible for MAPPA:

- *category 1* – offenders required to comply with the notification requirements of Part 2 of the 2003 Sexual Offences Act (see the Appendix for further details). These offenders are often referred to as being on the Sex Offender Register. The police have primary responsibility for identifying category 1 offenders.
- *category 2* – violent and other sexual offenders who have received a custodial sentence of 12 months or more since April 2001, a hospital or guardianship order, or who are subject to disqualification from working with children (2003 Criminal Justice Act, Section 327(3-5)). Responsibility for identifying category 2 offenders rests primarily with the probation service or YOTs.
- *category 3* – other offenders considered by the Responsible Authority to pose a 'risk of serious harm to the public' (2003 Criminal Justice Act, Section 325(2)). The criteria for category 3 are that:
  - The offender must have a conviction that indicates that they are capable of causing serious harm to the public.
  - The Responsible Authority must reasonably consider that the offender may cause harm to the public. The responsibility for identification lies with the agency that deals initially with the offender.

The local MAPPA coordinator in each area should be notified of all cases meeting the eligibility criteria for categories 1-3 (Ministry of Justice, 2007). The range of people eligible for MAPPA will be affected by any changes regarding registration requirements (category 1) and also trends in sentencing (category 2). Shifts towards tougher or more lenient sentencing will affect the number of offenders receiving custodial sentences of 12 months or more. Also, it should be noted that any bias in sentencing (for example on the grounds of ethnicity) could have a significant impact in terms of making certain groups more likely to come within the remit of MAPPA.

There are three levels of risk management within MAPPA (Ministry of Justice, 2007):

- *Level 1: Ordinary agency management* – where the risks posed by the offender can be managed by the agency responsible for supervision/case management of the offender. This does not mean that other agencies will not be involved: only that it is not considered necessary to refer the case to a level 2 or 3 MAPP meeting.
- *Level 2: Multi-agency public protection meeting* – for cases where the offender is assessed as presenting a high risk of serious harm to others and which requires active involvement and coordination of interventions to manage the presenting risks of harm.
- *Level 3: Multi-agency public protection meeting* – for cases that present risks that can only be managed by a plan that requires close cooperation at a senior level due to the complexity of the case and/or the unusual resource commitments involved. Level 3 may also be required in cases that, although not assessed as high or very high risk, attract considerable media and public attention and, as such, there is a need to ensure that confidence in the criminal justice system is maintained.

If an agency with responsibility for identifying MAPPA-eligible offenders (such as the probation service or a YOT) believes that the case can be appropriately managed at level 1, then they are required to *notify* the MAPPA coordinator and provide some basic information, but no more. In cases where it is felt that level 2 or 3 risk management is required, there must be a more detailed *referral*, which sets out the reasons why additional active multi-agency management may be required. Standardised notification and referral forms for use by all agencies involved in MAPPA are being introduced to help ensure greater consistency in this process.

The decision about which level of management is required in any given case will be based on an assessment of the risk of the offender causing serious harm to others and the factors influencing such judgements will vary in each case but '[t]he overriding principle is that cases should be managed at the lowest appropriate level, determined by defensible decision making' (Ministry of Justice, 2007, p 44). Lieb (2003, p 2) argues that one of the core tasks of MAPPA in relation to managing an individual offender is to 'anticipate how life changes may alter their risk' and risk management levels may therefore need to be altered (either up or down) as assessments of the risk that an offender presents change over time (Ministry of Justice, 2007).

Where an offender has been assessed as requiring multi-agency risk management, MAPPA have a responsibility to create 'individualized plans to mitigate this risk' (Lieb, 2003, p 2). Guidance also specifies that level 2 cases in the community should be reviewed every eight to 12 weeks, and level 3 cases every four to six weeks to 'ensure the risk management plan is effective and that the identified actions have been progressed' (Ministry of Justice, 2007, p 46). Where an offender is in custody, the process of setting the MAPPA level should take place at least six months prior to release so as to allow time for an appropriate risk management plan to be put in place. Information relating to offenders subject to MAPPA is recorded on the Violent and Sexual Offender Register (ViSOR) database, which is intended to be a 'central store for up-to-date information that can be accessed and updated by Police, Prisons (both public and private), Probation Services and, in the future, Youth Offending Teams' (Ministry of Justice, 2007, p 75).

YOTs and young people

This necessarily brief overview of MAPPA immediately suggests some questions about how these arrangements apply to young people. For example, if YOTs are already multi-agency organisations, can they be regarded as fulfilling MAPPA-type functions? Or, if risk levels in young people can fluctuate quickly and unpredictably – in view of the rapid changes that occur in behaviour during adolescence – would MAPPA be able to react to that appropriately?

Until recently, national MAPPA guidance tended to focus on adult offenders and paid relatively little attention to young people (see Sutherland, this volume). However, in response to questions and concerns about how MAPPA works with young people, including discussions at the symposium from which this book developed, a specific section on children and young people is now being added to the guidance (Ministry of Justice, forthcoming). In addition, the YJB has issued its own guidance on MAPPA (YJB, 2006), which sets out requirements for YOT practice in this area.

The key task for YOTs in their role as a 'duty to cooperate' agency is to identify young people who fall into one of the three categories outlined earlier and to have procedures in place for notification and referral of relevant cases to MAPPA. With regard to risk management, YOTs will normally be able to manage the majority of MAPPA-eligible cases at level 1 (Ministry of Justice, forthcoming). Despite their multi-agency status, however, YOTs cannot manage level 2 or 3 cases independently – any cases meeting these thresholds must be referred to MAPPA.

If a young person under YOT supervision is also a looked-after child, the local authority with responsibility for them should also be involved in MAPPA decision making. The guidance is clear that '[t]he YOT manager is not there to represent the Local Authority; this task should be undertaken by a different person' (Ministry of Justice, forthcoming), although at present there is little evidence to indicate the extent or level of local authority engagement with MAPPA for these cases.

In cases where a young person is assessed as requiring MAPPA level 2 or 3 risk management *and* has additional safeguarding needs, they could be referred to both MAPP and LSCB meetings as 'each has a separate and distinctive purpose' (Ministry of Justice, forthcoming). Where this occurs, the YOT case worker will have a pivotal role in ensuring that there is no duplication of effort or any conflict between the actions arising from each of the meetings.

At the time of writing, it is not clear how many young people are subject to MAPPA (and within that, which categories and levels they fall into) because MAPPA annual statistics have not previously reported on data by age. Sexual offences account for less than 1% of all offences committed by young people (YJB, 2007) so the number of young people in MAPPA category 1 will be relatively low. Given the recent increase in violent offending (YJB, 2007), it is likely that more young people will qualify for MAPPA via category 2 than category 1. More accurate data should be available in the future as SMBs are now expected to collect and monitor data on age in addition to ethnicity and gender (Ministry of Justice, 2007). As an approximation, however, it is estimated that around 2,000 young people are currently subject to MAPPA in England and Wales (Ministry of Justice, personal communication), with the majority of these being managed at level 1 (Sutherland and Jones, 2008).

Discussion

The ambivalence of society's current perceptions of, and attitudes towards, young people (Aynsley-Green, 2007; Thom et al, 2007) is magnified when it comes to questions about dealing with young people who offend. To give just one example, reconceptualising young people as agentic rather than passive (Sharland, 2006) and encouraging greater participatory rights for children may in fact 'reinforce the view that they should be treated more like adults with respect to the criminal law' (Lockyer et al, 2007, p 294) and perhaps lead to less attention being paid to their welfare.

This chapter has highlighted, first, the way in which different activities undertaken in the youth justice system – such as sentencing, assessments and interventions – all have to take account of risk, needs and rights. The way in which these interact is still unclear in many ways and 'little judicial scrutiny has been paid to the interplay between s37 of the Crime and Disorder Act and s44(1) of the Children and Young Person's Act' (Hollingsworth, 2007, p 169). The implications of this for organisational service delivery are thus open to debate.

These tensions become particularly acute when considering serious offending, particularly in the light of research evidence that indicates that young people who commit serious sexual and violent offences are often also vulnerable themselves (Boswell, 1996). The way in which states respond to children who offend and children who are in danger of being harmed varies considerably both between jurisdictions and within jurisdictions over time but in England and Wales (unlike Scotland) there has been an increasing bifurcation of youth justice and child protection systems in recent years (Hill et al, 2007).

This separation of young people as victims and young people as offenders is most apparent at the 'extremes', that is to say, MAPPA and LSCBs both deal with the most challenging cases. Thus, a young person committing minor offences and with few if any specific safeguarding concerns may receive a relatively integrated service from within the YOT, but in cases where more serious problems are identified then a young person is likely to be drawn into a range of different systems and procedures, which creates the potential for uncoordinated service delivery. While there may be advantages from having specific systems such as MAPPA and LSCBs to address different types of risk, this also raises concerns about the impact of a fragmented approach on those young people who are most likely to need consistent and coherent support from professionals. Youth Offending Teams therefore face a considerable challenge in ensuring that, at a systemic level, they engage effectively with a range of criminal justice and child protection services and, at individual case level, that practitioners help to ensure that young people receive as seamless a service as is possible within the current structure of youth justice.

A second important issue concerns the development of MAPPA and its 'fit' with the youth justice system. It has been argued that there is a trend towards the 'adulteration' (Muncie, 2007) of youth justice, particularly in relation to sentencing provisions (Easton and Piper, 2005), which erodes the longstanding principle that the criminal justice system should treat adults and young people differently. Could MAPPA be considered as an example of this process? Other contributors to this volume discuss such questions in more detail and the purpose of raising them here is more to initiate consideration of some of these critical questions.

Third, this chapter has highlighted the devolved nature of youth justice. With 157 locally accountable YOTs there will inevitably be challenges in implementing policy consistently and there is now also the additional complexity of adapting to the increasing divergence between England and Wales in relation to children's services provision. The YJB is limited in the extent to which it can direct practice from the centre and instead has to rely on providing guidance and training materials to help YOTs deliver services more effectively. Thus, although the legislation and guidance may appear clear in setting out how MAPPA should work, the localness of youth justice service provision can make implementation more difficult; for example, agreeing appropriate youth justice representation on SMBs can be complex when there may be many YOTs within one MAPPA area.

Fourth, is the emphasis on public protection – of which MAPPA is one significant part – contributing to the development of an unnecessarily complex criminal justice system? A striking example of this was seen in comments from the Court of Appeal describing the public protection sentencing provisions of the 2003 Criminal Justice Act as being so 'labyrinthine' that even judges struggled to understand them (*R v Lang and Ors* [2005] EWCA Crim 2864).[5] If criminal justice professionals find it difficult to understand some of the recent public protection initiatives, then how will young people and their parents or carers make sense of the system? There are important questions therefore as to how much young people understand about what MAPPA are and the implications of being identified as a MAPPA offender.

As these discussions illustrate, there is no easy way to respond to young people whose behaviour can present serious risks to others and who may also have complex needs themselves. 'Rather, any system has to balance a complex set of principles as well as an array of empirical evidence about the origin of childhood problems, the effectiveness of different kinds of intervention and the importance of inter-agency collaboration' (Lockyer et al, 2007, p 300). In applying this to youth justice in England and Wales, are MAPPA one example of how the criminal justice system 'neglects the best interests, needs and the welfare of children at the expense of protecting the public' (Aynsley-Green, 2007)? Or can they be a fair and constructive way of managing very difficult behaviour that contributes to the process of helping young people desist from serious offending, thus promoting both their interests and those of local communities? These and other dilemmas will be explored in more detail in the following chapters.

Notes

[1] In some areas, such teams are referred to as the Youth Offending Service but YOT is used throughout the book because this is the term referred to in the 1998 Act.

[2] The 2007 Local Government and Public Involvement in Health Act introduced significant changes in performance management processes at local area level.

[3] R (on the application of the Howard League) v Secretary of State for the Home Department and the Department of Health [2003] 1 FLR 484.

[4] As illustrated by the case of R (on the application of K) v Manchester City Council [2006] EWHC 3164 (Admin).

[5] See Stone (2005, 2006a, 2006b) for additional discussion of the complexity of sentencing in relation to young people who commit sexual offences and/or those coming within the 'dangerousness' provisions of the 2003 Criminal Justice Act.

References

Ashworth, A. (2007) 'Sentencing' in M. Maguire, R. Morgan and R. Reiner (eds) *The Oxford Handbook of Criminology* (4th edition, pp 990-1023), Oxford: Oxford University Press.

Aynsley-Green, Sir A. (2007) '11 million reflections on children in conflict with the law', lecture by the Children's Commissioner for England given at the Centre for Crime and Justice Studies, King's College, London, 27 November 2007, available from www.crimeandjustice.org.uk/

Baker, K. (2008) 'Sentencing young people', in M. Blyth, C. Wright and R. Newman (eds) *Young People and Custody*, Bristol: The Policy Press.

Boswell, G. (1996) *Young and Dangerous: The Backgrounds and Careers of Section 53 Offenders*, Aldershot: Avebury.

Bottoms, A. and Dignan, J. (2004) 'Youth justice in Great Britain', in M. Tonry and A. Doob (eds) *Youth Crime and Youth Justice: Comparative and Cross-National Perspectives*, London: University of Chicago Press.

Bottoms, A. and Kemp, V. (2007) 'The relationship between youth justice and child welfare in England and Wales', in M. Hill, A. Lockyer and F. Stone (eds) *Youth Justice and Child Protection*, London: Jessica Kingsley Publishers.

DCSF (Department for Children, Schools and Families) and the Ministry of Justice (2008) *Youth Crime Action Plan*, London: DCSF.

Easton, S. and Piper, C. (2005) *Sentencing and Punishment: The Quest for Justice*, Oxford: Oxford University Press.

Goldson, B. (2000) *The New Youth Justice*, Lyme Regis: Russell House Publishing.

Goldson, B. and Muncie, J. (2006) 'Rethinking youth justice: comparative analysis, international human rights and research evidence', *Youth Justice*, vol 6, no 2, pp 91-106.

Hill, M., Lockyer, A. and Stone, F. (2007) *Youth Justice and Child Protection*, London: Jessica Kingsley Publishers.

HM Government (2006) *Working Together to Safeguard Children*, London: The Stationery Office.

HM Government (2007) *Statutory Guidance on Making Arrangements to Safeguard and Promote the Welfare of Children under Section 11 of the Children Act 2004*, Nottingham: DfES Publications.

Hollingsworth, K. (2007) 'Protecting the rights of children leaving custody: *R (on the application of K) v Parole Board* and *R (on the application of K) v Manchester City Council*', *Journal of Social Welfare and Family Law*, vol 29, no 2, pp 163-75.

Kemshall, H., Parton, N., Walsh, M. and Waterson, J. (1997) 'Concepts of risk in relation to organizational structure and functioning within the personal social services and probation', *Social Policy & Administration*, vol 31, no 3, pp 213-32.

Lieb, A. (2003) 'Joined up worrying: the Multi-Agency Public Protection Panels', in A. Matravers (ed) *Sex Offenders in the Community: Managing and Reducing the Risks*, Cullompton: Willan.

Lockyer, A., Hill, M. and Stone, F. (2007) 'Conclusions', in M. Hill, A. Lockyer and F. Stone (eds) *Youth Justice and Child Protection* (pp 284-301), London: Jessica Kingsley Publishers.

Merrington, S. (2004) 'Assessment tools in probation: their development and potential', in R. Burnett and C. Roberts (eds) *What Works in Probation and Youth Justice: Developing Evidence Based Practice*, Cullompton: Willan.

Ministry of Justice (2007) *MAPPA Guidance Version 2.0*, National Offender Management Service, London: Ministry of Justice.

Ministry of Justice (forthcoming: 2009) *Children and Young People: Annex to MAPPA Guidance*, London: Ministry of Justice.

Morgan, R. and Newburn, T. (2007) 'Youth justice', in M. Maguire, R. Morgan and R. Reiner (eds) *The Oxford Handbook of Criminology* (4th edition, pp 292-321), Oxford: Oxford University Press.

Muncie, J. (2007) 'Adulteration', in B. Goldson (ed) *Dictionary of Youth Justice*, Cullompton: Willan.

NACRO (2006) *Guide to the Youth Justice System in England and Wales*, London: NACRO.

Newburn, T. (2002) 'Young people, crime and youth justice', in M. Maguire, R. Morgan and R. Reiner (eds) *The Oxford Handbook of Criminology* (3rd edition, pp 531-78), Oxford: Oxford University Press.

Pitts, J. (2001) *The New Politics of Youth Crime: Discipline or Solidarity*, Basingstoke: Macmillan.

Sentencing Guidelines Council (2008) *Dangerous Offenders: Guidance for Sentencers and Practitioners*, London: Sentencing Guidelines Council.

Sharland, E. (2006) 'Young people, risk taking and risk making: some thoughts for social work', *British Journal of Social Work*, vol 36, no 2, pp 247-65.

Solomon, E. and Garside, R. (2008) *Ten Years of Labour's Youth Justice Reforms: An Independent Audit*, London: Centre for Crime and Justice Studies.

Stone, N. (2005) 'Developments in sentencing young sexual offenders', *Youth Justice*, vol 5, no 2, pp 123-30.

Stone, N. (2006a) 'Entering the labyrinth: sentencing the dangerous young offender', *Youth Justice*, vol 6, no 1, pp 61-9.

Stone, N. (2006b) 'Into the labyrinth via the morass: issues for youth courts in dealing with gravity and dangerousness', *Youth Justice*, vol 6, no 2, pp 143-52.

Sutherland, A. and Jones, S. (2008) *MAPPA and Youth Justice: An Exploration of Youth Offending Team Engagement with Multi-Agency Public Protection Arrangements*, London: Youth Justice Board.

Thom, B., Sales, R. and Pearce, J. (2007) *Growing Up with Risk*, Bristol: The Policy Press.

YJB (Youth Justice Board) (2004a) *National Standards for Youth Justice Services 2004*, London: YJB.

YJB (2004b) *Sustaining the Success*, London: YJB.

YJB (2006) *Multi-Agency Public Protection Arrangements: Guidance for Youth Offending Teams*, London: YJB.

YJB (2007) *Youth Justice Annual Workload Data 2006/07*, London: YJB.

YJB (2008a) *Assessment, Planning Interventions and Supervision: Key Elements of Effective Practice*, London: YJB.

YJB (2008b) *Engaging with Young People: Key Elements of Effective Practice*, London: YJB.

2

MAPPA: learning the lessons for young offenders

Hazel Kemshall and Jason Wood

Introduction and context

The 1990s saw a growing preoccupation with high-risk offenders, particularly their accurate identification, reliable risk assessment and effective risk management. By the turn of the century this preoccupation had also extended to young offenders, and included the formalised use of risk assessment tools and increasing attention to the early identification of those young offenders likely to become 'dangerous' (see Kemshall, 2008a, for a full review). A key component of the policy and organisational response to high-risk offenders was the development of the Multi-Agency Public Protection Arrangements (MAPPA) (see Kemshall, 2003, for a full review). By the late 1990s, MAPPA extended across England and Wales (with slightly later developments in Scotland and Northern Ireland). These arrangements were given legislative force in the 2000 Criminal Justice and Court Services Act (Sections 67 and 68) with the police and the probation service forming 'Responsible Authorities' (and the prison service being added as a statutory partner by the 2003 Criminal Justice Act. MAPPA are tasked with making 'joint arrangements for the assessment and management of the risks posed by sexual and violent offenders, and other offenders who may cause serious harm to the public' (Home Office, 2001, p 1).

MAPPA have been characterised as a 'community protection model' (Connelly and Williamson, 2000). This model is embedded in the criminal justice system and is characterised by the use of restriction, surveillance, monitoring and control, compulsory treatment and the prioritisation of victim/community rights over those of offenders. Special measures such as licence conditions, tagging, exclusions, registers and selective incarceration are all extensively used (Kemshall, 2001, 2003; Kemshall et al, 2005). Risk management plans are devised and delivered by statutory agencies in partnership (Home Office, 2004; Ministry of Justice, 2007). Youth Offending Teams (YOTs) come within the remit of MAPPA and were designated a 'duty to cooperate' agency by the 2003 Criminal Justice Act. This places a duty on YOTs to cooperate with MAPPA in the risk assessment and management of high-risk offenders (see YJB, 2006a, 2006b).

These developments can be placed within a broader penal trend usually referred to as the 'new penology' of risk or 'actuarial justice' (Feeley and Simon, 1992, 1994), although the extent and nature of the new penology has been the subject of much debate (see, for example, O'Malley, 2001; Rigakos and Hadden, 2001; Kemshall, 2002, 2003). In essence, the proponents of the new penology contend that actuarial justice is driven both by economic concerns to risk-manage and sentence effectively and by social concerns to regulate the 'dangerous classes' and 'habitual recidivists' (Pratt, 1997, 2000). While there is continued debate about the role of risk in criminology, crime control and penal policy (Kemshall, 2003; O'Malley, 2006), there is little doubt that risk has become a significant factor in responses to crime, including youth crime (Goldson, 2000; Kelly, 2000, 2001; Muncie, 2006; Kemshall, 2008a).

Protection through partnership has also been a significant driver since the 1990s and such partnerships were given impetus and legal force by the 1998 Crime and Disorder Act (Sections 115-17), the 2000 Criminal Justice and Court Services Act and the 2003 Criminal Justice Act. Partnership is seen as an important 'value-added' component to work with high-risk offenders, offering efficient and effective information exchange, quality risk assessment and additional resources for risk management.

Key areas of MAPPA research

MAPPA in various forms have been in existence since the mid-1990s and have been subject to various research evaluations of performance. Extensive research for the Home Office (see Kemshall and Maguire, 2001; Maguire et al, 2001) between November 1998 and October 1999 found varying degrees of formal cooperation, differing systems and processes, differing risk assessment tools in use and differing definitions of high-risk offenders. Risk management plans were also variable, and it was not always clear that risk management interventions were matched to the levels and types of risk identified. Subjective, 'professional' judgements often replaced actuarial tools, especially within the panel discussions, and as a consequence risk thresholds and categories were a moveable feast (see Maguire et al, 2001, for a full review). These issues were subsequently addressed by policy (Home Office, 2003) and legislation (the 2000 Criminal Justice and Court Services Act, Sections 67 and 68). A further MAPPA evaluation (Kemshall et al, 2005) found some improvement in practice, but also a number of remaining issues. This research (commissioned by the Home Office) carried out a national questionnaire survey of all the MAPPA areas supported by in-depth fieldwork in six areas (see Kemshall et al, 2005, for a full review of the methodology). The research examined key areas of MAPPA practice, processes and structures, and made recommendations for improving practice nationally – a number of which have been subsequently implemented in the 2003 Criminal Justice Act and further guidance (Home Office, 2004). The research concluded that there is 'evidence of greater effectiveness and consistency across MAPPAs' (Kemshall et al, 2005, p 2) and that the 'majority of areas considered they were "effective" or "very effective" at identifying the "critical few" offenders and in classifying them appropriately' (2005, p 22). This improved effectiveness rested on improved referral processes to MAPPA, more effective systems for risk assessment including the use of tools such as the adult Offender Assessment System (OASys) and Risk Matrix 2000, and structured assessment discussions at panels.

This second MAPPA evaluation also considered MAPPA practice in respect of young offenders. With one or two notable exceptions, YOTs were not well embedded into the MAPPA structure. Few referrals to MAPPA were being made, and YOT managers and workers struggled to see the relevance and 'value-added' of MAPPA to their work. Cases falling within the MAPPA criteria were seen to be few, and MAPPA were consequently viewed as time consuming and resource intensive for the benefits provided. Discerning benefits was particularly difficult for YOTs given that they were already working within a multi-agency context with routine access to the police, health and social services. Therefore, the benefits of information exchange and additional resources for risk management were seen as limited (Kemshall et al, 2005, pp 21-3).

This 2005 evaluation also confirmed previous research by Baker et al (2003), which identified worker confusion about the role and use of the risk of serious harm section of *Asset* (the risk assessment tool for young offenders), with 'many staff seeing it as a method indicating a young person's vulnerability rather than the risk posed by the young person to others' (Kemshall et al, 2005, p 21). This prompted further guidance from the Youth Justice Board for England and Wales (YJB) (see YJB, 2006b), although there was some confusion between the risk of harm and the risk of reoffending (see YJB, 2005, for an example of this confusion). There is limited evidence of the impact of the guidance on the management of dangerous offenders and the operation of MAPPA. While it was supported by practice guidance on risk (Wilkinson and Baker, 2005) and extensive training (personal experience of the author), fieldwork on risk and crime pathways from 2001 to 2005 (see Kemshall et al, 2006; Boeck et al, 2006) found risk characterised by YOT workers as predominantly vulnerability and need (Kemshall, 2007). Consequently, it has been suggested that '[t]he coverage of the tools, and often their emphasis upon risk, prevention and control, has affected the commitment of workers to their use' (Kemshall, 2007, p 10).

A recent evaluation of MAPPA performance – *MAPPA – The First Five Years* (Home Office, 2007) – has indicated general success for public protection panels. The report noted that the number of serious further offences committed by offenders managed at levels 2 and 3 in 2005/06 was only 0.44%. The biggest impact of MAPPA on recidivism was at level 3, 'and such a low serious re-offending rate for this particular group of offenders is to be welcomed and supports the view that MAPPA is making a real contribution to the management of dangerousness in the community' (Home Office, 2007, pp 6-7). Unfortunately, figures for young offenders subject to MAPPA were not available (and are still not routinely collected), thus it is difficult to comment on MAPPA effectiveness with young offenders.

However, key issues from research into MAPPA work with adult offenders have transferability to work with young offenders. Kemshall et al (2005) found that poor or non-completion of risk assessment tools hindered appropriate referrals to MAPPA and the efficient and effective assessment of risk by public protection panels. The work of public protection panels is also adversely affected by poor information exchange, and the evaluation report recommended a 'minimum standard' for information packages:

- a full risk assessment by the referring agency;
- key characteristics of the offender including any 'local knowledge' about the offender (based on evidential rather than anecdotal information);
- prison information, if available (for example, discipline record, response to treatment programmes, key contacts and correspondence, psychologist report, parole report);
- previous response to supervision and any previous convictions noted by the police (Kemshall et al, 2005, p 13).

This is reflected in the YJB MAPPA guidance in the section covering what is required for a MAPPA referral (YJB, 2006b, p 10). However, as Nash (2007, p 91) succinctly puts it:

> Effective assessment of risk is dependent not only upon gathering as much information as possible, but also on making the *best* use of it. It also requires a constant updating of the information and analysis, especially in the case of young offenders who may be changing and developing at a rapid rate.

In addition to rapid change, young offenders may be difficult to 'know', particularly if presenting early in their criminal careers, or without significant patterns of sexual or violent behaviour. This presents particular challenges, which are addressed in the next section.

Risk assessment of young offenders for MAPPA

High-risk young offenders may present with a limited 'track record' of offending and little or no custodial experience, and those young offenders who commit a 'grave crime'[1] early in their careers present particular assessment issues (Boswell, 1997, 1999, 2000, 2007). Boswell found that within her sample of one third of the Section 53 population (young people who had been sentenced to life imprisonment) (sample = 200), 72% had experienced one or more kinds of abuse: physical 40%, sexual 29%, emotional 28.5%, organised/ritual 1.5% or combinations of abuse 27% (Boswell, 2007, p 46). Fifty-seven per cent had experienced a significant bereavement or loss of contact with a parent. Significantly, she states that: '[t]he total number who had experienced both abuse and loss was 35%, suggesting that the presence of a double trauma may be a potent factor in the lives of young people who offend violently'

(Boswell, 2007, p 46). Similar results were found by Falshaw and Browne (1997), Hamilton et al (2002), Falshaw (2005) and Lösel and Bender (2006). However, it must be stressed that not all children who experience abuse and loss will become violent offenders, and young offenders who commit a serious or 'grave crime' *as a first offence* do not necessarily go on to commit further offences of this type (Bailey, 1996; Boswell, 1997, 1999, 2007). This distinguishes them from those young offenders who progress through other types of violent crime and for whom past violent behaviour continues to be the best predictor of future violent behaviour. Early identification of potentially violent offenders has proved problematic, as has the concept of 'career' for such offenders. However, early aggressiveness and its continuation throughout childhood appear to be an indicator of future violent offending (Farrington, 1995, 1998; Farrington and West, 1993). It is also important to note that young offenders who commit serious violent offences are not necessarily specialists, and do commit other offences (Farrington, 1995, 1998).

The *Asset* risk of harm section considers the following to be key factors in the identification of cases of concern:

- evidence of any harm-related behaviour by the young person, including behaviour under preparation, particular victim characteristics, offender factors and the results of any harmful behaviour (including any unintentional results);
- pattern, frequency and severity of harmful behaviour;
- current static and dynamic risk indicators;
- assessment of future harmful behaviour (*Asset*: Risk of Serious Harm: Full Assessment; YJB, 2006c).

This information will need to be supplemented by a full 'pen picture' of the young person, including any information about trauma, abuse and victimisation, and is addressed by the YJB MAPPA guidance (YJB, 2006b, pp 8, 10).

Risk management

Research has also highlighted challenges in the risk management of offenders by MAPPA, most notably the appropriate matching of plans to risk factors, and in sustaining effective risk management plans over time (Kemshall et al, 2005; Wood and Kemshall, 2007). Good planning is critical to effective risk management, and public protection panels have a critical role in ensuring this. The 2005 evaluation noted the following as essential to good risk management planning:

- proactive and relevant information exchange;
- a full picture of the offender's circumstances, a full risk assessment and details of known or potential victims;
- a systematic review of risk factors and identification of potential trigger factors and circumstances under which risk might escalate;

- clearly defined actions to match the critical risk factors and how these actions are likely to reduce risk;
- allocation of agency and worker responsibility for actions with clear timelines;
- contingency plan in the event of a breakdown (summarised from Kemshall et al, 2005, p 14).

These standards are easily transferable to young offenders discussed at MAPPA, and are reflected in the YJB MAPPA guidance on planning (YJB, 2006b, p 11). However, young offenders cannot be treated simply as 'mini adults' and interventions should have regard to levels of maturity, learning capacity and the social skill level of children and adolescents.[2] Cognitive behavioural programmes should be age appropriate, sensitive to the learning style of the young person, supported by appropriate motivational work and followed up by reinforcement of key lessons learned (Kemshall, 2007).

A traditional learning style is likely to be inappropriate for many young offenders, as many of them will have had unsatisfactory experiences in school. Interventions with young people need to recognise the developmental stage of the individual, encourage them to make positive choices and balance the management of risk to the young person against the risks they pose to others (Hill et al, 1991; Borduin et al, 1995).

It is also important to recognise that children and young people do not necessarily experience their lives as a source of risk, nor do they necessarily see themselves as posers of risks to others. Problematic behaviours and risk taking may be framed positively and seen as both rewarding and justified and corrective action by adult-led institutions can be both resisted and resented. Recent studies have shown young people as proactive risk takers (Boeck et al, 2006; Kemshall et al, 2006), capable of constructing alternative selves to those framed by policy (Kemshall, 2008a) and capable of negotiating risk and adverse circumstances contrary to current risk prevention predictions (Ungar, 2007). Young people's behaviour that may seem by outsiders as 'deviant' may in fact be navigation strategies that young people employ in order to ward off greater risks. For example, 'street life' may be a tactic to avoid risks at home, or peer associations may be a strategy to seek protection in groups in locations where territorial disputes are common (Wood, 2008).

The study by Boeck et al (2006) also found that young people can be prudential about the risks they face and take, although not always in the ways adults might expect. Young people were well able to display a calculative attitude to risk, weighing costs and benefits, the desirability of particular outcomes and could express intentionality in their actions. However, they also recognised the constraints on acting prudentially, for example, restrictions on their choice, the speed with which some decisions are made, describing some risky decisions as 'spur of the moment' and that some risks are 'accidents and not planned at all'. Interestingly, adults were seen as a group who should be more prudential, but who often weren't, for example by drink driving, exposing young people to risks (for example by giving school detentions that meant they had to walk home alone in the dark) or committing illegal activities in front of them. Prudentialism was also seen as contingent, dependent on the likely outcome of the risk (how big it might be), whether or not it was illegal and whether or not the behaviour was age dependent (for example smoking). This resonated with previous research that emphasised young people's accounts of risk and decision making, and saw their 'risk taking behaviour as grounded within the specific social and economic context in which they live' (Mitchell et al, 2001, p 218). While such decision making is often characterised as irrational by official and policy-driven accounts of risk, close attention to young people's framing of risk can often show them as 'expert "risk" managers and survivors' (Mitchell et al, 2001, p 218). These 'situated vocabularies' of risk (Mitchell et al, 2001, p 218) are potentially a rich source of data on how young people are regularly assessing and managing risk. There is a growing body of research literature in this area, focusing on health risks (for example drug use and smoking; Denscombe, 2001), crime risks (Kemshall, 2003) and general risks associated with 'youth' (MacDonald and Marsh, 2001).

While official discourse may characterise many of these behaviours as 'irrational' (Armstrong, 2004), Denscombe (2001) found that whether something is perceived as a risk and whether risks are taken can depend on the priorities of the young person and the meaning they attach to the risky behaviour. Taking risks can be crucial to the self-identify of the young person (Denscombe, 2001) and can depend on the perceived social benefits to the young person of taking the risks (for example membership of a group). Children and young people do not necessarily see risk in the same way as adults (Furlong and Cartmel, 1997; France, 2000), although their views on this dissonance can be sophisticated. For example, they can point to instances where adults perform in just the same way as themselves in relation to well-known risks such as alcohol consumption or smoking.

Against this background, workers may struggle to encourage young people to reframe their risk-taking behaviours and cognitive behavioural programmes focusing on 'right thinking' may have a limited impact. Young people may resent the imposition of 'corrective thinking' when from their standpoint they are thinking straight and making perfectly rational decisions about risk.

Also, to be prudent you have to have a notion of the future, what it might be like and how your own actions can influence it. However, for some young people, being prudential about the future is seen as pointless; their lives are lived almost exclusively in the present. In fact, in one study they exhibited a somewhat fatalistic attitude to their futures, possibly reflecting their sense of hopelessness:

> I think it is better to just take each day as it is and see what happens.

> Yes live for today and not for tomorrow.

> Because if you are relying on one thing then you are going to get stressed out and you will have a shit life anyway.

It is a bit hard to aim here, I am not thinking about it anymore because when I get back to reality it really pees me off. (Boeck et al, 2006)

Interestingly, this fatalistic attitude to the future framed approaches to risk. In essence, respondents perceived that they had little to lose (that is, to risk) and this reframed any calculative approach to risk decisions. Interestingly, this resulted in a more 'cavalier' and reckless attitude to committing crime, but a rather risk-averse attitude to leaving established peer groups and the immediate locale to take up other opportunities. Incentives to change were seen as limited and unrewarding and the potential losses attached to changing networks, activities and behaviours were seen as high. This can make 'moving on from crime' seem costly, risky and too challenging.

Public protection panels need to be aware of these challenging issues in the management of young offenders. Some MAPPA areas have developed specialist panels to discuss such cases, particularly at level 2. These panels can usefully provide a young person focus and specialist disciplinary knowledge. However, they can also function as 'shadow panels' without proper regulation and with poor standards of assessment and management practice (see Sutherland and Jones, 2008). This is exacerbated where the criteria for risk levels are inappropriately applied, and cases are inflated into MAPPA beyond their risk level, resulting in 'net widening' and the operation of a 'precautionary' 'better safe than sorry' attitude to difficult (but not always risky) cases (Kemshall et al, 2005). This finding was replicated by Sutherland and Jones (2008) evaluation of MAPPA and young people, and can be adequately addressed by guidance, standard setting for referrals and risk-level criteria, and quality assurance of level 2 panels (Kemshall et al, 2005).

As well as identifying risk factors, it is important to identify protective factors that can counteract negative influences. Interventions should aim to strengthen and develop these protective factors alongside other measures to promote external and internal controls. Resilience is not merely the opposite of risk, and protective factors are not merely the inverse of risk factors. While protective factors are broadly understood as any influence that ameliorates or reduces risk, causally linking particular protective factors to particular risks has proved difficult (Garmezy, 1993; Hackett, 2005). The cumulative effect of protective factors is seen as important although which factors, how to weight them and how they interact is less clear. This has led more recent commentators to consider protection as a process, and protective factors have been extended into the notion of 'resilience', with research increasingly interested in why some children are resilient to adversity and why others are not (Schoon and Bynner, 2003; Kemshall et al, 2006; Schoon, 2006; Thom et al, 2007; Kemshall, 2008a). Resilience requires resources and social capital to work, for example access to significant, pro-social adults, stability and continuity through life's transitions (see, for example, Newman and Blackburn, 2002; Newman, 2004). This also illustrates the importance of trust in adults, continuity of supervision and the quality of relationships with workers.

Pro-social supervision and discretionary disclosure

Recent work has identified a 'pro-social' approach with offenders (including high-risk ones) as helpful in reducing reoffending (Rex, 1999; Trotter, 2000, 2007; McNeill and Batchelor, 2002), and includes the supervision of 'young, high-risk, violent and drug-using offenders' (McNeill and Batchelor, 2002, p 38). This pro-social approach is underpinned by an assumption that offenders, if given the opportunities to engage effectively, can and will change behaviours in most cases. Pro-social modelling comprises:

- being clear about the supervisory role, including purpose and expectations of supervision, the appropriate use of authority and the role of enforcement;
- clear expectations about required values and behaviours and their reinforcement through the use of rewards;
- challenge and confrontation of undesirable behaviours and the discouragement of pro-criminal attitudes and values;
- negotiated problem solving, clear objective setting, monitoring and accountability of the offender's progress;
- an honest, empathic relationship with an emphasis on persistence and a belief in the offender's capacity to change (adapted from Trotter, 1999, 2000, 2007; McNeill and Batchelor, 2002, p 38).

In an in-depth evaluation of good practice in three MAPPA areas, Wood and Kemshall (2007) found that the balance between external and internal controls was the key to effective risk management. Various external controls were employed, including legal requirements, parole conditions, curfews, exclusion zones, residence requirements and the use of unannounced home visiting. While some offenders saw external controls as intrusive, where they could perceive a link between such controls and the management of their behaviour they were more likely to accept and comply with them. In one MAPPA area, this approach was supported by the use of contracts with offenders, and while not legally binding, these provided an important starting point for supervision and engaged offenders in planning their own risk management. Engaging the offender and emphasising the 'good lives' model (Ward and Maruna, 2007; McNeill, this volume) underpinned the best practice observed in the study, with one area achieving success in reintegrating sex offenders back into housing, employment and, for young sex offenders, education. The careful use of discretionary disclosure also assisted offender re-integration, including young offenders back into schools, colleges and youth groups. Discretionary disclosure allows for the disclosure of information about an offender to a third party. The rules governing disclosure are covered in the MAPPA guidance (Home Office, paras 93-5) and the essential criteria for such a decision to be made are presented in para 95:

i) the offender presents a risk of serious harm to the person, or to those for whom the recipient of the information has responsibility (children for example);

ii) there is no other practicable, less intrusive means of protecting the individual(s), and failure to disclose would put them in danger. Also, only that information which is necessary to prevent the harm may be disclosed, which will rarely be all the information available;

iii) the risk to the offender should be considered although it should not outweigh the potential risk to others were disclosure not to be made. The offender retains his rights (most importantly his Article 2 right to life) and consideration must be given to whether those rights are endangered as a consequence of the disclosure. It is partly in respect of such consideration that widespread disclosure of the identity and whereabouts of an offender is very, very rarely if ever justified;

iv) the disclosure is to the right person and that they understand the confidential and sensitive nature of the information they have received. The right person will be the person who needs to know in order to avoid or prevent the risks;

v) consider consulting the offender about the proposed disclosure. This should be done in all cases unless to do so would not be safe or appropriate. Where consultation can be done, it can help strengthen the risk management plan. If it is possible and appropriate to obtain the offender's consent then a number of potential objections to the disclosure are overcome. Equally, the offender may wish to leave the placement rather than have any disclosure made, and if this is appropriate, this would also avoid the need for any disclosure;

vi) ensure that whoever has been given the information knows what to do with it. Again, where this is a specific person, this may be less problematic but in the case of an employer, for example, you may need to provide advice and support; and

vii) before actually disclosing the information, particularly to an employer or someone in a similar position, first ask them whether they have any information about the offender. If they have the information then no disclosure is necessary. If they have some but possibly incorrect information your disclosure can helpfully correct it. (Home Office, 2004, para 95)

Discretionary disclosure, or 'controlled disclosure' as practitioners call it, is made primarily to employers, accommodation providers, church groups and school and college staff. Interestingly, most controlled disclosure is carried out with the consent of the offender, either by the offender themselves at the instigation of the supervising officer, or by the supervisor on the offender's behalf. In in-depth interviews with offenders subject to MAPPA, offenders were quite aware of the need to disclose and recognised that this will be routinely done on a need-to-know basis, for example to youth group leaders or teachers (Wood and Kemshall, 2007; Kemshall and Wood, 2008). The procedure ensures public safety, informal supervision, some community reintegration and support, and minimal risk of vigilante action. Such an approach also appears to realistically balance public protection with a limited guarantee of privacy for the offender – a limit that most offenders interviewed understood and accepted (Wood and Kemshall, 2007; Kemshall and Wood, 2008).

Balanced risk management

Increasingly, evaluations and research are promoting balanced risk management as the most effective strategy with high-risk offenders, and particularly with young offenders (Bailey et al, 2007; Boswell, 2007; Kemshall, 2007; Wood and Kemshall, 2007; Kemshall, 2008b). Such plans attempt to balance rehabilitative aims with restrictions, surveillance and monitoring techniques. In the in-depth interviews mentioned above, Wood and Kemshall (2007) found that offenders valued and benefited from attention to their personal and social problems, and to their personal goals, needs and desire – an approach promoted by the 'Good Lives Model' (see Ward and Stewart, 2003a, 2003b). The feelings of loyalty, commitment and accountability that offenders had to their probation officer/worker were also important in ensuring compliance and commitment to the change process, and compliance with intrusive restrictive conditions such as curfews, residence requirements and exclusion zones (Wood and Kemshall, 2007). Similar findings have been presented in respect of young offenders, with work by McNeill and Batchelor in particular (2002, 2004) emphasising the importance of a quality relationship between worker and young person in which the worker can help the young person make sense of the change process and enhance their commitment to the intervention (see also Farrow et al, 2007, p 71). Holistic risk management packages need to both focus on the triggers for risky behaviours and also enhance protective factors and build resilience. This can include attention to 'human capital' – personal resources and self-efficacy for avoiding risk, assisting young people in making 'better' decisions on risk (see Farrall, 2002, 2004) – but also the social capital and resources required to escape offending circumstances and literally create a new, non-offending lifestyle (Boeck et al, 2006). This can include the role of trusted and consistent adults, assistance with key life transitions and access to pro-social networks (Boeck et al, 2006; Kemshall, 2008a).

Conclusion: the critical success factors

MAPPA depends on the robust and rigorous exchange of information and the genuine multidisciplinary contribution of panels to discussion and assessment (Kemshall et al, 2005; Nash, 2007). Youth Offending Teams should not necessarily presume that they have routine access to this within their own team structures. As Sheldrick (1999, p 509) points out, the strength of a multi-agency approach is in the difference and range of perspectives present, and where groups become homogeneous in their views they risk operating without a critical edge and without the richness of differing disciplinary views. Given the close and routine working relationships of YOTs, there is a risk of insularity and homogeneity, and public protection panels offer scrutiny, challenge and transparency to difficult and challenging decisions. Effective decision making is also dependent on accurate and reliable assessments of the risk of harm, and urgent attention should be given to the standard of current assessments of young offenders (see Baker, 2008). Such assessments need to include attention to key triggers and risk factors, including abuse, trauma and victimisation. Panels may also assist with devising and implementing balanced and holistic risk management plans and also assist with safe reintegration into local communities and groups particularly where controlled disclosure is required.

In addition, YOTs need to be properly embedded within MAPPA, with specialist panels at level 2 regulated and quality assured to avoid net-widening and inconsistency (a point supported by current YJB MAPPA guidance; see YJB, 2006b). Wood and Kemshall (2007) found that offenders can accept and comply with MAPPA risk management plans if they are explained properly, have a clear rationale about safety, are supported by pro-social supervisors and have their own legitimate needs met. There are potential benefits for young people where MAPPA operate rigorously, not least the prevention of net-widening, high-quality holistic risk assessments and balanced risk management plans (particularly for those suffering trauma, abuse and loss). For this latter group in particular, MAPPA may provide access to scarce but highly desirable resources (see Hackett et al, 2003, for deficits in service delivery to young people who sexually abuse).

MAPPA responses to young offenders can learn a lot from research predominantly with adult offenders, but importantly, such responses must take account of recent research into 'what works' with young offenders, particularly high-risk violent and sexual offenders. While young offenders are not 'mini adults', they can and do benefit from MAPPA, but MAPPA must also work sensitively and with care with young people.

Notes

[1] For example, those crimes committed by an offender aged between 10 and 17, which, if committed by an adult, would be punishable by 14 years or more in prison (Sections 90 and 91 of the 2000 Powers of Criminal Courts [Sentencing] Act and Section 61 of the 2000 Criminal Justice and Courts Act).

[2] The Department of Health and the Dartington Research Unit have provided a maturation guide in *Looking After Children: Assessment and Action Records* (Dartington Research Unit, 1995) based on health, education, identity, relationships, social presentation, emotional and behavioural development and self-care skills.

References

Armstrong, D. (2004) 'A risky business? Research, policy and governmentality and youth offending', *Youth Justice*, vol 4, no 2, pp 100-16.

Bailey, S. (1996) 'Adolescents who murder', *Journal of Adolescence*, vol 19, no 1, pp 19-39.

Bailey, S., Vermeiren, R. and Mitchell, P. (2007) 'Mental health, risk and antisocial behaviour in young offenders: challenges and opportunities', in M. Blyth, E. Solomon and K. Baker (eds) *Young People and 'Risk'* (pp 53-76), Bristol: The Policy Press.

Baker, K. (2008) 'Risk, uncertainty and public protection: assessment of young people who offend', *British Journal of Social Work*, vol 38, no 8, pp 1463-80.

Baker, K., Jones, S., Roberts, C. and Merrington, S. (2003) *Validity and Reliability of Asset: Findings from the First Two Years of the Use of ASSET*, London: YJB, available from www.yjb.gov.uk/publications

Boeck, T., Fleming, J. and Kemshall, H. (2006) 'The context of risk decisions: does social capital make a difference?', *Forum: Qualitative Social Research*, vol 7, no 1, article 17, available from www.qualitative-research.net/fqs-texte/1-06/06-1-17-e.htm

Borduin, C.M., Mann, B.J., Cone, L.T., Henggeler, S.W., Fucci, B.R., Blaske, D.M. and Williams, R.A.(1995) 'Multi-systemic treatment of serious juvenile offenders: long-term prevention of criminality and violence', *Journal of Consulting and Criminal Psychology*, vol 63, no 4, pp 569-78.

Boswell, G. (1997) 'The backgrounds of violent young offenders: the present picture', in V. Varma (ed) *Violence in Children and Adolescents* (pp 22-36), London: Jessica Kingsley Publishers.

Boswell, G. (1999) 'Young offenders who commit grave crimes: the criminal justice response', in H. Kemshall and J. Pritchard (eds) *Good Practice in Working with Violence* (pp 33-49), London: Jessica Kingsley Publishers.

Boswell, G. (2000) *Violent Children and Adolescents: Asking the Reasons Why*, London: Whurr.

Boswell, G. (2007) 'Young people and violence: balancing public protection with meeting needs', in M. Blyth, E. Solomon and K. Baker (eds) *Young People and 'Risk'* (pp 39-52), Bristol: The Policy Press.

Connelly, C. and Williamson, S. (2000) *Review of the Research Literature on Serious Violent and Sexual Offenders*, Crime and Criminal Justice Research Findings No 46, Edinburgh: Scottish Executive Central Research Unit.

Dartington Research Unit (1995) *Looking After Children: Assessment and Action Records* (revised version), London: HMSO.

Denscombe, M. (2001) 'Uncertain identities and health-risking behaviour: the case of young people and smoking in late modernity', *British Journal of Sociology*, vol 52, no 1, pp 157-77.

Falshaw, L. (2005) 'The link between a history of maltreatment and subsequent offending behaviour', *Probation Journal*, vol 52, no 4, pp 423-34.

Falshaw, L. and Browne, K. (1997) 'Adverse childhood experiences and violent acts of young people in secure accommodation', *Journal of Mental Health*, vol 6, no 5, pp 443-56.

Farrall, S. (2002) *Rethinking What Works with Offenders: Probation, Social Context, and Desistance from Crime*, Cullompton: Willan.

Farrall, S. (2004) 'Social capital and offender reintegration: making probation desistance focused', in S. Maruna and R. Immarigeon (eds) *After Crime and Punishment*, Cullompton: Willan.

Farrington, D.P. (1995) 'The development of offending and antisocial behaviour from childhood: key findings from the Cambridge Study in Delinquent Development', *Journal of Child Psychology and Psychiatry*, vol 36, no 6, pp 929-64.

Farrington, D.P. (1998) 'Predictors, causes, and correlates of male youth violence', in M. Tonry and M.H. Moore (eds) *Youth Violence* (pp 421-72), Chicago, IL: University of Chicago Press.

Farrington, D.P. and West, D. (1993) 'Criminal, penal and life histories of chronic offenders: risk and protective factors and early identification', *Criminal Behaviour and Mental Health*, vol 3, no 4, pp 492-523.

Farrow, K., Kelly, G. and Wilkinson, B. (2007) *Offenders in Focus: Risk, Responsivity and Diversity*, Bristol: The Policy Press.

Feeley, M. and Simon, J. (1992) 'The new penology: notes on the emerging strategy for corrections', *Criminology*, vol 30, no 4, pp 449-75.

Feeley, M. and Simon, J. (1994) 'Actuarial justice: the emerging new criminal law', in D. Nelken (ed) *The Futures of Criminology* (pp 173-201), London: Sage Publications.

France, A. (2000) 'Towards a sociological understanding of youth and their risk taking', *Journal of Youth Studies*, vol 3, no 3, pp 317-31.

Furlong, A. and Cartmel, F. (1997) *Young People and Social Change: Individualization and Risk in Late Modernity*, Buckingham: Open University Press.

Garmezy, N. (1993) 'Vulnerability and resilience', in D. Funder and R. Parke (eds) *Studying Lives Through Time: Personality and Development* (pp 377-98), Washington, DC: American Psychological Association.

Goldson, B. (2000) '"Children in need" or "young offenders"? Hardening ideology, organizational change and new challenges for social work with children in trouble', *Child and Family Social Work*, vol 5, no 3, pp 255-65.

Hackett, S. (2005) 'Risk and resilience: two sides of the same coin', Presentation to the Risk Assessment and Child Protection Conference, Bonnington Hotel, London, 22 March.

Hackett, S., Masson, H. and Phillips, S. (2003) *Mapping and Exploring Services for Young People who have Sexually Abused Others*, London: NSPCC, available from www. nspcc.or.g.uk/inform

Hamilton, C.E., Falshaw, L. and Browne, K. (2002) 'The link between recurrent maltreatment and offending behaviour', *International Journal of Offender Therapy*, vol 46, no 1, pp 75-94.

Hill, J., Andrews, D.A. and Hoge, R.D. (1991) 'Meta-analysis of treatment programs for young offenders: the effect of clinically relevant treatment on recidivism, with controls for various methodological variables', *Canadian Journal of Program Evaluation*, vol 6, no 1, pp 97-109.

Home Office (2001) *Initial Guidance to the Police and Probation Services on Sections 67 and 68 of the Criminal Justice and Court Services Act 2000*, London: Home Office.

Home Office (2003) *MAPPA Guidance Version 1.0*, London: Home Office.

Home Office (2004) *MAPPA Guidance Version 1.2*, London: Home Office.

Home Office (2007) *MAPPA – The First Five Years: A National Overview of the Multi-Agency Public Protection Arrangements 2001-2006*, London: Home Office.

Kelly, P. (2000) 'Youth as an artefact of expertise: problematising the practice of youth studies', *Journal of Youth Studies*, vol 3, no 3, pp 301-15.

Kelly, P. (2001) 'Youth at risk: processes of individualisation and responsibilisation in the risk society', *Discourse: Studies in the Cultural Politics of Education*, vol 22, no 1, pp 23-33.

Kemshall, H. (2001) *Risk Assessment and Management of Known Sexual and Violent Offenders: A Review of Current Issues*, Police Research Series Paper 140, London: Home Office.

Kemshall, H. (2002) 'Effective practice in probation: an example of "advanced liberal responsibilisation"?', *The Howard Journal*, vol 41, no 1, pp 41-58.

Kemshall, H. (2003) *Understanding Risk in Criminal Justice*, Buckingham: Open University Press.

Kemshall, H. (2007) 'Risk assessment and risk management: the right approach?', in M. Blyth, E. Solomon and K. Baker (eds) *Young People and 'Risk'* (pp 7-24), Bristol: The Policy Press.

Kemshall, H. (2008a) 'Risks, rights and justice: understanding and responding to youth risk', *Youth Justice*, vol 8, no 1, pp 21-37.

Kemshall, H. (2008b) *Understanding the Community Management of High Risk Offenders*, Maidenhead: Open University Press/McGraw-Hill.

Kemshall, H. and Maguire, M. (2001) 'Public protection, partnership and risk penality: the multi-agency risk management of sexual and violent offenders', *Punishment and Society*, vol 3, no 2, pp 237-64.

Kemshall, H. and Wood, J. (2008) 'Partnership for public protection: key issues in the multi-agency public protection arrangements (MAPPA)', in C. Clark and J. McGhee (eds) *Private and Confidential? Handling Personal Information in Social and Health Services* (pp 111-128), Bristol: The Policy Press.

Kemshall, H., Mackenzie, G., Wood, J., Bailey, R. and Yates, J. (2005) *Strengthening the Multi-Agency Public Protection Arrangements*, London: Home Office.

Kemshall, H., Marsland, L., Boeck, T. and Dunkerton, L. (2006) 'Young people, pathways and crime: beyond risk factors', *Australian and New Zealand Journal of Criminology*, vol 39, no 3, pp 354-70.

Lösel, F. and Bender, D. (2006) 'Risk factors for serious violent antisocial behaviour in children and youth', in A. Hagell and R. Jeyarajah-Dent (eds) *Children who Commit Acts of Serious Interpersonal Violence: Messages for Best Practice* (pp 42-72), London: Jessica Kingsley Publishers.

MacDonald, R. and Marsh, J. (2001) 'Disconnected youth?', *Journal of Youth Studies*, vol 4, no 4, pp 373-91.

McNeill, F. and Batchelor, S. (2002) 'Chaos, containment and change: responding to persistent offending by young people', *Youth Justice*, vol 2, no 1, pp 27-43.

McNeill, F. and Batchelor, S. (2004) *Persistent Offending by Young People: Developing Practice*, Issues in Community and Criminal Justice Monograph No 3, London: NAPO.

Maguire, M., Kemshall, H., Noaks, L. and Wincup, E. (2001) *Risk Management of Sexual and Violent Offenders: The Work of Public Protection Panels*, Police Research Paper No 139, London: Home Office.

Ministry of Justice (2007) *MAPPA Guidance Version 2.0*, National Offender Management Service, London: Ministry of Justice.

Mitchell, W., Crawshaw, P., Bunton, R. and Green, E. (2001) 'Situating young people's experience of risk and identity', *Health, Risk and Society*, vol 3, no 2, pp 217-34.

Muncie, J. (2006) 'Governing young people: coherence and contradiction in contemporary youth justice', *Critical Social Policy*, vol 26, no 4, pp 770-93.

Nash, M. (2007) 'Working with young people in a culture of public protection', in M. Blyth, E. Solomon and K. Baker (eds) *Young People and 'Risk'* (pp 85-95), Bristol: The Policy Press.

Newman, T. (2004) *What Works in Building Resilience*, Ilford: Barnados.

Newman, T. and Blackburn, S. (2002) *Transitions in the Lives of Children and Young People: Resilience Factors*, Edinburgh: Scottish Executive, available at www.scotland.gov.uk/library5/education/ic78-00.asp

O'Malley, P. (2001) 'Discontinuity, government and risk', *Theoretical Criminology*, vol 5, no 1, pp 85-92.

O'Malley, P. (2006) 'Criminology and risk', in G. Mythen and S. Walklate (eds) *Beyond the Risk Society: Critical Reflections on Risk and Human Security* (pp 43-59), Maidenhead: Open University Press.

Pratt, J. (1997) *Governing the Dangerous*, Sydney: Federation Press.

Pratt, J. (2000) 'The return of the wheelbarrow men: or, the arrival of postmodern penality?', *British Journal of Criminology*, vol 40, no 1, pp 127-45.

Rex, S. (1999) 'Desistance from offending: experiences of probation', *Howard Journal of Criminal Justice*, vol 38, no 4, pp 366-83.

Rigakos, G. and Hadden, R.W. (2001) 'Crime, capitalism and the "risk society": towards the same old modernity?', *Theoretical Criminology*, vol 5, no 1, pp 61-84.

Schoon, I. (2006) *Risk and Resilience: Adaptation in Changing Times*, Cambridge: Cambridge University Press.

Schoon, I. and Bynner, J. (2003) 'Risk and resilience in the life course: implications for interventions in social policies', *Journal of Youth Studies*, vol 6, no 1, pp 21-31.

Sheldrick, C. (1999) 'Practitioner review: the assessment and management of risk in adolescents', *Journal of Child Psychiatry*, vol 40, no 4, pp 507-18.

Sutherland, A. and Jones, S. (2008) *MAPPA and Youth Justice: An Exploration of Youth Offending Team Engagement with Multi-Agency Public Protection Arrangements*, London: YJB.

Thom, B., Sales, R. and Pearce, J. (2007) *Growing Up with Risk*, Bristol: The Policy Press.

Trotter, C. (1999) *Working with Involuntary Clients: A Guide to Practice*, London: Sage Publications.

Trotter, C. (2000) 'Social work education, pro-social orientation and effective probation practice', *Probation Journal*, vol 47, no 4, pp 256-61.

Trotter, C. (2007) 'Pro-social modelling', in G. McIvor and P. Raynor (eds) *Developments in Social Work with Offenders* (pp 212-33), Research Highlights No 48, London: Jessica Kingsley Publishers.

Ungar, M. (2007) *Too Safe for their Own Good: How Risk and Responsibility Help Teens Thrive*, Toronto: McClelland and Stewart.

Ward, T. and Maruna, S. (2007) *Rehabilitation (Key Ideas in Criminology)*, London: Routledge.

Ward, T. and Stewart, C. (2003a) 'Criminogenic needs and human needs: a theoretical model', *Psychology, Crime and Law*, vol 31, no 3, pp 282-305.

Ward, T. and Stewart, C. (2003b) 'The treatment of sex offenders: risk management and good lives', *Professional Psychology: Research and Practice*, vol 34, no 4, pp 353-60.

Wilkinson, B. and Baker, K. (2005) *Managing Risk in the Community* (1st edition), London: YJB.

Wood, J. (2008) 'Young people and active citizenship: an investigation', PhD thesis, De Montfort University.

Wood, J. and Kemshall, H., with Maguire, M., Hudson, K. and Mackenzie, G. (2007) *The Operation and Experience of Multi-Agency Public Protection Arrangements*, London: Home Office.

YJB (Youth Justice Board) (2005) *Risk and Protective Factors*, London: YJB.

YJB (2006a) *Criminal Justice Act 2003: 'Dangerousness' and the New Sentences for Public Protection (Guidance for Youth Offending Teams)*, London: YJB, available from www.yjb.gov.uk/publications

YJB (2006b) *Multi-Agency Public Protection Arrangements: Guidance for YOTs*, London: YJB, available from www.yjb.gov.uk/publications

YJB (2006c) *Asset: Risk of Serious Harm: Full Assessment*, London: YJB, available from www.yjb.gov.uk/publications

3

Youth Offending Teams and MAPPA: past problems, current challenges and future prospects

Alex Sutherland[1]

'I've never seen a young person's case be brought before a MAPPA meeting, despite having attended a gazillion of them. And that worries me as a practitioner who obviously would be seeing these young people … or potentially would be seeing these young people in … a year or two's time.' (Probation officer, symposium participant)

Introduction

This chapter focuses on why there may be practical difficulties for Youth Offending Teams (YOTs) and those running Multi-Agency Public Protection Arrangements (MAPPA) to work alongside one another, stemming from both historical trends and differing occupational cultures. This is not to say that all YOTs have problems working within the MAPPA framework; anecdotally we know that many YOTs operate very successfully in this area. However, the impression gathered from YOTs that took part in a recent research project (hereafter termed the Oxford MAPPA study) and reports from participants in a subsequent symposium was that this relationship can be problematic, and setting out some possible reasons for this forms the basis of this chapter.

The first part of this chapter outlines the Oxford MAPPA study, presenting the main findings and discussing some of the limitations of the research. Following on from this, the second part of the chapter presents a brief history of YOTs and MAPPA, drawn from available research and guidance. This section goes on to present a number of possible explanations for difficulties in YOT–MAPPA engagement. Recommendations from the Oxford MAPPA study are presented, with an emphasis on why these were made and what they hoped to accomplish, alongside a realisation that more thought needs to be given to issues beyond simply the process and administration of risk management in this context. The conclusion underlines the need for YOTs to be involved with MAPPA, on the basis that their absence means a body of knowledge about young people will be missing from the process.

The Oxford MAPPA study

Study methodology and aims

Early delays and difficulties in the study meant that gaining basic information was problematic and that the original (and broader) aims had to be revised. As a result, the study sought to:

- record how many young people were subject to MAPPA in England and Wales;
- explore what constitutes 'best practice' in YOT–MAPPA relations; and
- examine how local practice in YOTs varies from national guidance.

An email-based survey was sent to all YOT managers and MAPPA coordinators asking for the category and level of all young people currently included within the MAPPA framework. These requests yielded information from 83 of 157 YOTs in England and Wales (53%), accounting for approximately 1,000 young people subject to MAPPA in these areas. It was not possible to obtain a breakdown by ethnic group or gender of these figures from YOTs or the Public Protection Unit (PPU) so questions over diversity cannot be answered at this stage. Equally, while some work has been undertaken to profile adult MAPPA cases (Wood, 2006), there is a gap in knowledge in relation to the specific risk/need profiles of young people subject to MAPPA. The second element of the project was a number of case studies, exploring how YOTs engaged with MAPPA. Seven YOTs (of eight approached) were visited and 13 interviews were undertaken with managers and senior practitioners. In addition, during the course of collecting survey data, numerous discussions with MAPPA coordinators and YOT managers took place and additional information was supplied on the survey forms.

Study limitations and findings

There were practical difficulties and methodological limitations to the study. The first of these was that the email survey was dogged by delays and those completing it frequently reported that the information they collected was incomplete (or compiled by less than rigorous means). The primary limitations of the study were that the representativeness of survey and interview data could not be established. However, the seven YOTs that participated in the detailed case study elements of the research might be regarded as 'typical', in that if something occurs in one of these YOTs it could occur anywhere. The seven YOTs presented the research team with broad variations in practice from which it could be argued that logical (if not empirical) generalisations can be made about the operation of MAPPA more widely (Patton, 1990, pp 174-5).

Bearing these limitations in mind, the study produced a number of findings. First, MAPPA coordinators and YOT managers had difficulties providing accurate information on the numbers of young people currently subject to MAPPA. Second, at least one of the YOTs in the study was working under the assumption that it was able to manage cases at level 2 without reference to MAPPA. Third, two YOTs reported that the high volume of adult MAPPA cases in the local area had resulted in tacit or explicit requests not to notify the MAPPA coordinator about young people unless they were above a certain threshold of seriousness/risk. In addition, at least one YOT reported that the local MAPPA had their own criteria for notifying cases in addition to those included in the MAPPA guidance. It was suggested that the creation of extra criteria might be a result of individuals who repeatedly attend MAPP meetings becoming desensitised to variations in risk levels (see 'High-risk cases and risk fatigue', p 52, this volume). Fourth, two YOTs reported that local and national initiatives aimed at persistent offenders – Priority and Prolific Offender (PPO) schemes and Intensive Supervision and Surveillance Programmes (ISSPs) – were being used as diversions from MAPPA (in the case of PPO) or (for ISSPs) were being used as a 'standard' form of supervision for every MAPPA case (see Sutherland and Jones, 2008). The use of such schemes as either diversionary or as a form of default supervision means that they are not being used as intended and that the net of the ISSP has widened further (see Moore et al, 2006; Sutherland et al, 2007). The use of the ISSP as default supervision also diverges from what is regarded as best practice in the form of 'what works' principles, notably risk classification – where the intensity of an intervention is matched to the risk of reoffending (McGuire, 1995).

Finally, YOTs reported inconsistencies in what constitutes the different MAPPA risk management levels and this seems to have resulted in areas within England and Wales that differ widely in how risks are perceived and managed (Sutherland and Jones, 2008). These inconsistencies mirror some of the findings from Kemshall et al (2005) who found wide variation in the:

- definition and application of categories (and subsequent referral to MAPPA) by YOTs;
- representation of YOTs at MAPP meetings;
- ways in which YOTs manage level 2 and 3 cases (Kemshall et al, 2005, pp 14-15).

In concluding their report, Sutherland and Jones (2008) point out the similarities between the issues being faced by YOTs now and the early days of MAPPA and probation (see Kemshall, 2001), and suggest that:

> If YOTs are on similar 'practice pathways' … particular attention should be given to the research evidence relating to probation … which show[s] that many improvements in the system have been made as the result of a great deal of work by both the probation service and central government. If YOTs are to mitigate the problems highlighted in this report, it seems that a logical first step would be to understand what is already known about MAPPA and use this knowledge to continue improving practice. (Sutherland and Jones, 2008, pp 37-8)

YOTs and MAPPA

There is very little commentary on the relationship between YOTs and MAPPA. Two exceptions are that of Bryan and Doyle (2003) who give a view from the 'inside' on the creation of MAPPA and the first year of operation (and who mention but do not detail YOT involvement); and Lieb (2003) who briefly discusses this issue when reviewing the proposals for setting up MAPPA and the first annual reports. Lieb notes (2003, p 214) that, in some areas, MAPPA explicitly 'decided not to handle young offenders [because] the majority of young people do not pose a serious risk of harm to the public'. Another probation area delegated responsibility entirely to the YOT and one further set a minimum age limit for consideration of 16 for all YOT cases.[2]

The reviews of MAPPA completed by Maguire et al (2001) and Kemshall et al (2005) could not, by the nature of the work (primarily looking at MAPPA in an adult context), spend a great deal of time discussing the vicissitudes of probation practice and give the same detailed treatment to YOTs. The study of MAPPA and YOTs by Sutherland and Jones (2008) goes some way to describing the operation of MAPPA by YOTs, but as discussed earlier, the research only detailed work in seven teams and only offers a recent view of this practice.

Some idea of the position of YOTs within MAPPA can be gained by examining the MAPPA guidance. Initial documentation sent out to the police and the probation service about the implementation of Section 67 and 68 of the 2000 Criminal Justice and Court Services Act (Home Office, 2001) does not mention YOTs. Neither does the first version of the MAPPA guidance (Home Office, 2003) other than stating that they are a 'duty to cooperate' agency. The second version of the MAPPA guidance (Home Office, 2004) expands on this and states that 'YOTs are multi-agency partnerships in which police and probation play an important role ... [and that] [t]he Responsible Authority should regard YOTs as performing the "single agency" risk assessment and risk management at MAPPA Level I' (Home Office, 2004, p 83). Reflecting pressure from the YJB, the most recent version of the Ministry of Justice guidance contains many more references to YOTs and details that:

> The YJB recognises that an important part of the Duty to Co-operate upon YOTs requires them to agree the process, by which young people for whom the YOT has supervisory responsibility and who meet the relevant eligibility criteria, are referred to MAPPA. YOTs will undertake a comprehensive risk assessment on all cases referred to MAPPA. (Ministry of Justice, 2007, p 94)

For the first time, some discussion is offered as to the position of young people and MAPPA, with the guidance suggesting that:

> The number of young offenders meeting the MAPPA eligibility criteria will be relatively small. Identifying the level of risk presented by a young person can be particularly difficult given that they may have a limited criminal history and that patterns of

behaviour can often change rapidly during adolescence. However ... there are a small number of young people who present a serious risk to others and for whom a multi-agency intervention may therefore be required. (Ministry of Justice, 2007, p 26)

On the surface, the early commentary from Lieb (2003), findings from Kemshall et al (2005) and the later research by Sutherland and Jones (2008) suggest that some YOTs (at the very least the ones included in these studies), have found it difficult to work with MAPPA since its inception in 2001/02. There are a number of possible reasons for this, which will be considered in the following sections, namely that:

(1) YOTs have only been in existence since 2000. As such, their remit and organisation were still underdeveloped so they were not in a position to be involved in MAPPA during the early stages.
(2) There are very few crimes being committed by young people of the nature that concerns MAPP meetings.
(3) The initial exclusion of YOTs from MAPPA reflects ongoing occupational tension between YOTs and MAPPA.

YOTs as new organisations

Proposition 1 is that, as similar findings were reported by Kemshall et al (2005) and Sutherland and Jones (2008), this suggests that if YOTs being new was a reasonable position in 2003/04 (when the Kemshall et al research was conducted), it cannot be a justification for the findings from the later Oxford study. We should also consider the fact that early on in the days of MAPPA, young people who committed specified offences and who received 12 months or more on a Detention and Training Order (DTO) or in custody under the 2000 Criminal Justice and Court Services Act were deemed to be 'relevant sexual or violent offenders' for the purpose of that Act. This means that when YOTs were introduced in 2000, a small proportion of their caseload would have been eligible for MAPPA. Given this, it might be suggested that because YOTs were new and because some of their cases would have been eligible for MAPPA they should have been more involved from the moment they were operational. Perhaps these early cases were not on the YOT radar because of the heavy focus on adult offenders within MAPPA at the time.

Serious offending is rare

Proposition 2 is that young people simply do not commit many crimes that would qualify them for MAPPA. For category 1 cases (sex offences), there are over 70 offences that, if convicted, warrant further consideration for notification or referral (primarily by the police) to MAPPA. However, not all of those committing a sexual offence will have to be listed on the Sex Offender Register (YJB, 2006). In some instances (for example taking indecent photographs of children under 16), those aged under 18 must receive 12 months (or more) imprisonment (or a 12-month DTO) before they have to register and would thus be notified or referred to MAPPA (see the Appendix). For other offences (for example rape), registration is automatic. In some specific instances where the age of the offender is not deemed relevant (for example in cases of abuse of position of trust), registration is required if the offender received 'a prison sentence; was detained in hospital; or was made the subject of a 12 month [or longer] community sentence' (YJB, 2006, p 18).

For category 2 cases (violent and other sexual offences), the offences that trigger notification or referral are also contingent on receiving a custodial sentence (or DTO) of 12 months or more. But it must not be forgotten that many of those who commit a violent offence will not receive the minimum 12-month custodial sentence. Overall, only around 3.3% of all disposals at court result in a custodial sentence (YJB, 2007). Of the 6,702 young people who were released from prison in 2007/08, only 403 (6%) had served a sentence of 12 months or more (YJB, personal communication).

The final group of MAPPA eligible cases (category 3) are 'other persons who, by reason of offences committed by them (wherever committed), are considered by the Responsible Authority to be persons who may cause serious harm to the public' (2003 Criminal Justice Act, Section 325(2)(b)). For an individual to be considered under this category, they must have previously committed an offence which demonstrates that they present a risk of serious harm to others. In addition, the Responsible Authority (not the YOT, although they can refer the case), must believe that the individual currently presents a risk of serious harm to others. In practice, those coming into MAPPA via category 3 will (most likely) be individuals who have previously been supervised under MAPPA in categories 1 and 2 and/or those who have committed an offence that, when combined with other information, leads to a concern for public safety (for example a young person burgles a house but takes only underwear). However, even with a relevant offence 'the Responsible Authority must have reason to believe that the offender may cause serious harm to the public' (YJB, 2006, p 7).

Overall, while the number of eligible *offences* committed may number in the thousands, the number of *individuals* who would actually qualify on the basis of their offence *and* the sentencing requirement is very small. Thus, proposition 2 goes some way in explaining why some areas have more involvement with MAPPA than others: a low incidence rate would mean limited exposure to the process and/or need to engage and understand it.

Occupational tension between YOTs and MAPPA

Proposition 3 would also account for the (apparent) lack of initial engagement with MAPPA. We can take as evidence of this initial exclusion (a) the lack of discussion in both the earlier versions of MAPPA guidance (Home Office, 2003, 2004) and (b) the absence of YOTs from the reviews and commentaries undertaken. The next section attempts to provide broader explanations for the difficulties encountered by YOT engagement with MAPPA. It offers some explanation as to why MAPPA coordinators and partner agencies may lack confidence in dealing with YOTs and may find it difficult to involve them in the MAPPA process.

YOTs as protectors of the public

As Jones and Baker (this volume) have set out, YOTs are subject to a range of statutory obligations – in essence they have two hats to wear in relation to both *public* and *child* protection. As such, YOTs must juggle obligations to prevent offending and protect the public, while also having a mind for the rights and welfare of the young person who has offended (see Whitty, this volume). This juggling act perhaps sets YOTs apart from other criminal justice agencies in terms of the number of balls they have in the air at once.

Owing to these responsibilities to both the public and the child, it would be reasonable to suggest that most (if not all) YOTs are averse to 'ratcheting up' the risks associated with young people. Within the context of MAPPA, this might translate into a hesitancy to refer cases resulting from a (perceived or real) conflict between welfare and public protection considerations. However, YOTs also want (need?) to be taken seriously by the agencies that constitute MAPP meetings and thus face a dilemma within the context of the 'risk game'. To be accepted in this arena, YOT practitioners and managers have to adopt the language, practice and culture of MAPPA, characterised as being one of punishment and control (Nash, 2007). This may be at odds with what used to be considered a more social work ethos within YOTs (see studies by Burnett and Appleton, 2004; Ellis and Boden, 2005). However, since the publication of these studies a great deal has changed within YOTs in terms of an increasing focus on risk and public protection, alongside their welfare remit, but an understanding of this shift may not have yet filtered through to partner agencies. Operating within MAPPA presents YOTs and the partner agencies (primarily the police and probation), with a number of issues for cooperation and practice which are set out below.

YOTs as less predictable risk assessors

Lieb (2003, pp 213-14) sets out how alliances between business partners rely on trust, but begin with 'uncertainty about partners' motives'. If we extend this idea to the two hats hypothesis set out in the section above, then problems with YOT engagement in MAPPA might be understandable. If YOTs participate in MAPP meetings without clearly stating their obligations (for example, reducing reoffending, public protection, child welfare, child protection) then they might be viewed as 'youth probation' with the same emphasis on public protection and compliance, whereas there is a distinction between what YOTs and the probation service deliver (see Morgan and Newburn, 2007; Nash, 2007). If YOTs, in their engagement with MAPPA, neglect the last two of these obligations then continued participation would become difficult. For example, if the public protection hat is given prominence by a YOT participant, then later objections from the YOT about invasive management under MAPPA, based for instance on human rights (in particular children's rights – see Whitty, this volume) or legal obligations arising from welfare legislation (see Jones and Baker, this volume), might be harder to vocalise. On the other hand, those workers who place child welfare/protection (in relation to the individual offender) above public protection might run into accusations of not taking public protection seriously (or the more common political quip of not being tough enough). Uncertainty about the remit of YOT work could mean that agencies with more clearly defined parameters for public protection (for example the police) and less concern with the 'rights of the offender' might be less inclined to take on YOT assessments of risk or indeed engage with the wider YOT agenda.

Furthermore, in a situation with so much potential expert knowledge to follow, Haggerty (2003, p 201, citing Hunt) points out that the decision about who to listen to '[has] to be made, like so many other lifestyle choices, on the basis of subjective preferences whose roots and motivations we are rarely able to perceive'. For instance, the location of the police as a key 'risk profession' in the risk society (Ericson and Haggerty, 1997) means that they are viewed as occupying 'a pivotal role in making risks visible, and advising and instructing on their management' (Campbell, 2004, p 696). Within MAPPA, the police and the probation service have historically been central in decision making. As a result, a police (or probation) officer may be more convincing and persuasive in their representation of risk than a YOT worker or manager in this context.

Furthermore, there is an anecdotal view from within the probation service that YOTs are not as 'good' or 'knowledgeable' about assessing risk as those with a probation background are. One probation officer at the symposium suggested that some probation staff question 'whether [YOT] officers think about risk in the same way probation officers do … and they question the training the YOT officers get, and think of it as a little sister, as a poor relative'. As one MAPPA coordinator suggested, 'YOTs are more child protection agencies' (symposium participant). This view was strongly rebutted by a YOT manager who stated that it was 'out of date' to think about YOTs as child protection agencies and that they are 'public protection agencies … that manage [the] balance'. It is interesting to note that such a vociferous objection was made, and the way it was put – it seems unlikely that the same would have occurred even a few years ago, such has the change been in the focus of YOT work. This is perhaps best highlighted by the recent drive by the YJB towards a 'risk-based' approach (YJB, 2008), which is an explicit move towards making risk management the central enterprise of youth justice. Despite this shift, it might be argued that YOTs cannot alter their training to inculcate all new staff with 'risk' to the extent that the probation service has done (see Bailey et al, 2007; Burnett et al, 2007) because YOTs have a wider range of responsibilities than other criminal justice agencies.

Cosy thinking

While there has been a shift in the focus of YOT work to include public protection and risk management in a more formalised way, such a shift is not without problems. Youth Offending Teams are already multi-agency organisations, which include representatives from the police and the probation service (among others). Having a team with wide-ranging expertise and knowledge from backgrounds that mirror those of the agencies involved in MAPPA could lead some YOTs to operate in the belief that they do not need to refer cases to MAPP meetings. Sutherland and Jones (2008) encountered three (of seven) YOTs who believed that they did not have to refer level 2 cases because the YOTs in question were already multi-agency. Furthermore, in another example, at least one YOT was largely disengaged from the MAPPA process and had created its own 'shadow' arrangements, which ran without any oversight from, or involvement with, the local MAPPA coordinator. While the latter is an extreme case, instances where the YOT believes in its effectiveness as a multi-agency partnership could result in 'cosy thinking' about the ability of the YOT to assess and recognise risk. The YOT worker might, for instance, think that 'all the agencies in the YOT don't think this individual is dangerous, they are from the same agencies as the MAPP meeting, so it must be an equitable assessment to that which the panel would make'. Likewise, a YOT worker might engage in 'risk minimisation' where the potential for harm committed by a young person is downplayed ('we know about young people, we know about risk of serious harm and we know that young people are not dangerous').

Even when cases are referred to a MAPP meeting, YOTs may believe that MAPPA add little to what they already do ('rubber stamping' as one senior practitioner put it in Sutherland and Jones, 2008, p 24). Kemshall and Wood (this volume) have highlighted that MAPPA are dependent on the 'robust and rigorous exchange of information and the genuine multidisciplinary contribution of panels to discussion and assessment'. A well-thought-out risk management plan, which is able to utilise the agencies represented within the YOT, might only receive a rubber stamp of approval from the MAPP meeting. Unless the YOT is told why no amendments were made (for example because the plan is already as good as it needs to be), it would be hard to motivate YOT staff to engage with a process that they view as bureaucratic. The more times rubber stamping occurs without a qualification of the decision by the MAPP meeting, the harder it seems to resist the idea that practitioners and/ or managers would begin to 'get cosy' in their thinking and possibly question the necessity for notification and referral.

Examples from child protection highlight the problems of insular thinking about risk. The 'satanic abuse' cases in Cleveland, Nottingham, the Orkney Isles and Rochdale spanned from the latter part of the 1980s into the new millennium. These cases saw groups of social workers remove children from their families because they (wrongly) believed that ritual abuse was taking place, primarily based on evidence gathered from the children alone (for example, Nottinghamshire Social Services, 1990; see

Munro, 1999, for more on decision making in child protection). One has to wonder if a contemporaneous external review of these accusations by a body equivalent to MAPPA could have prevented these cases from being forced through (against court rulings in some instances). Thus, the requirement for notification or referral to the MAPP meeting has the benefit of a fresh pair of eyes looking at the information on the case. In essence, being compelled to submit to such an external review (or even of the prospect of it) may prompt YOTs to break patterns (habits) of thinking about their risk assessment procedures and/or young people.

High-risk cases and risk fatigue

MAPP meetings rely on risk assessments completed by partner agencies, and the combination of these with experiential knowledge means that decisions in MAPPA are (necessarily) more clinical than actuarial in nature (for the time being). Clinical decision making, even when well regulated, carries with it the possibility of bias and error. Those who are constantly working in a culture of clinical decision making on high-risk cases may eventually normalise the risks they encounter and evaluate because of what has been termed 'risk fatigue' (Sutherland and Jones, 2008, p 30).

The phrase 'risk fatigue' has been used in other contexts to refer to the overloading of the public with messages about risk in general (Adams, 2003) and dietary health in particular (Eckersley, 2001). In both of these instances, it is used to describe a state of apathy towards risks related to drinking or eating too much and 'a state of cynicism engendered by the popular media's habit of sensationalizing every newly discovered virtual risk' (Adams, 2003, p 98). Within a criminal justice context, it is suggested here that the continued presence of the same individuals at MAPP meetings may result in them being unable to recognise more finely grained constructions of risk, such as those presented by someone who is young. Yet, this may not be confined to MAPPA. Many YOTs have introduced 'high-risk' teams who only deal with serious and/or persistent cases. Will individuals on such teams be able to recognise the antecedents of serious offending if their perceptions are geared towards individuals who already present a risk of serious harm, or will they dismiss such cases until the unthinkable happens?

Legislation and risk context as factors in decision making

In thinking about risk fatigue in a high-risk context, more thought can be given to that milieu as an influence on how decisions are made. Baker (this volume) presents a range of important factors relating to decision making within MAPPA. However, the issues of professionalism, different conceptualisations of risk and the understanding/ use of discretion are nested within broader factors that may directly influence the way in which YOTs interact with the MAPPA process. The first of these is the legislative framework. New offences are created and extraordinary controls are instituted on existing offenders, often as a result of public pressure, fears about 'security' and moral panics. While these shifts may go unnoticed by the general populace, they mean real changes at the front line where more and more individuals are brought under the remit of public protection ('widening the net'). This puts a strain on the agencies and professionals involved (Nash, 2006), increasing the pressure to make decisions (perhaps too?) quickly.

However, legislation merely sets the limits of who should be considered. During the Oxford MAPPA study (and also in Kemshall and colleagues' work), it was clear that there were inconsistencies in both the understanding of MAPPA and the application of this knowledge. Between the seven YOTs visited by Sutherland and Jones (and those who responded to the questionnaire), there was wide variation in both implementation and practice even within coterminous probation areas (see Sutherland and Jones, 2008, pp 21-4). Some of the difficulties faced may in part be due to the different resource pressures YOTs have; not all YOTs will have MAPPA-eligible cases, whereas others will have many cases that fit the criteria. However, the throughput of juvenile cases may only be a footnote when the local adult offender population is considered alongside it. Youth Offending Teams may have many cases that require referral based on risk assessments, but when compared to the local adult population, young people seem less 'risky' and thus may not be referred.

> I think inevitably ... there will be a comparison ... but then I guess [the local MAPPA] have certain thresholds and criteria and they're interested in the most dangerous. A lot of the young people we work with aren't the most dangerous compared to [adults] ... maybe that's partly because obviously they haven't got the history of convictions. ... there are threshold issues. (YOT senior practitioner) (Sutherland and Jones, 2008, p 30)

Bennett (2008) highlights that a recent publication on the efficacy of the adult Offender Assessment System (OASys) showed 'significant variation' in practitioner assessments of risk of serious harm. Bennett reports this as an indication of inconsistency in practice. An alternative viewpoint (and one that became clear in Sutherland and Jones, 2008) is that regional differences in the 'seriousness caseload' may affect practitioner perceptions of what is 'really serious' (that is, what requires *referral* to MAPPA) and how this is assessed; and what is 'standard' probation/YOT work (which might require *notification* but nothing further):

> [T]his is maybe because of the sort of context that we operate in ... a 12 year old with a knife just doesn't raise any interest in me at all. You know it's absolutely bog standard ... I would expect all the practitioners to be able to deal with that as a run of the mill case ... it wouldn't even meet our internal risk warning systems. (symposium participant, 2008)

There are two overlapping factors for determining the risk context that can be derived from this brief discussion. The first factor is the *volume of juvenile cases:* more cases equates to a greater likelihood that a young person will both commit an offence and receive the appropriate sentence for notification/referral. The second factor is the *seriousness of both the probation service and YOT caseloads.* If the local probation service caseload is top heavy (that is, with many serious offenders), this will set the bar higher for acceptance at level 2 or level 3 by the local MAPP meetings. Likewise, if the YOT caseload is top heavy the threshold for referral to MAPPA for level 2 or 3 may also be higher, as cases that might on paper warrant referral will be 'bog standard' YOT work in that area (imagine and compare the typical composition of caseloads in Manchester or Inner London with rural Yorkshire or mid-Wales). The result of these threshold-raising factors is that the local risk context results in '(relatively) very high and very low risk areas across England and Wales' (Sutherland and Jones, 2008, p 35).

Discussion

The condition of youth is one of uncertainty where change is frequent and influences are manifold. Young people are different from adults in a number of important ways and, as such, they must be treated differently; a point that has been made not only in relation to MAPPA (Kemshall and Wood, this volume; Monk, this volume) but also to drug treatment (Hayes, 2004). The result of this distinction is that those who only have experience of adult risk might not be able to think about risk and young people. Youth Offending Team engagement with MAPPA is therefore crucial as the YOT practitioner/manager brings with them a body of knowledge that may be missing from otherwise adult-focused MAPP meetings. As one YOT manager put it, 'my concern is whether the right people are in the room who understand the young people' (YOT performance manager, symposium participant). If this is the case, then when faced with a referral for a young person (as one senior probation officer noted about their chairing of MAPP meetings) 'the people at the table don't necessarily think "this is a child" and ... invariably don't have an understanding of the [2004] Children Act and of safeguarding' (symposium participant). The absence of this knowledge could lead to a poor level of notification and/or referral by YOTs, poor risk assessment and ultimately poor risk management decisions.

> [The probation service] don't sort of work with young people, they don't know what services we've got. So they've come in to chair a meeting not knowing sort of what services we've got, what it offers to young people, and how we work with young people really. (Deputy YOT manager, formerly senior probation officer) (Sutherland and Jones, 2008, p 31)

As with trying to engage young people, there may be innumerable factors that influence successful participation. Thinking about cases in isolation from dissimilar others (making more reasonable comparisons); avoiding stereotyping young people as low risk (either from 'cosy thinking' or 'risk fatigue'); and maintaining a good exchange of information, are all required to make MAPPA work. Underlying all of these is the fact that the MAPPA process has to be concerned with the individual offender (qua individual; see McNeill, this volume). Risk management is about what needs to be in place to allow practitioners to work with the *individual* to manage risk of serious harm and reoffending. In managing their own risks (becoming 'responsibilised'; Kemshall, 2002), individuals become aware of what triggers their offending, of what the 'danger signs' are, and learn how to avoid these triggers or manage their behaviour in more socially acceptable ways. Young people, as a distinct but far from homogenous group, may require handling with kid gloves (that is, with care and sensitivity), but this may be hard to realise when they commit acts that seem un-childlike.

Recommendations from the Oxford MAPPA study

In response to the issues discovered during their research, and despite the limitations of the project, Sutherland and Jones (2008, p 36) were able to suggest a number of recommendations for the YJB and PPU.

In the first instance, it was clear that neither YOTs nor MAPPA coordinators were aware of how many young people were subject to MAPPA. It was also apparent that YOTs were unclear about notification requirements for MAPPA. To this end, three recommendations were made, which suggested that clarification be given to both YOTs and MAPPA coordinators about notification and referral requirements and the role of YOTs (specifically that they cannot manage level 2 cases independently without reference to MAPPA). It was also suggested that MAPPA status might become a monitoring requirement for YOTs and returns be collated centrally by the YJB. In the interim between report writing and publication, the PPU began requesting information for annual reports on the age of young people referred or notified to MAPPA. However, the fact remains that this is only an annual exercise and individual coordinators and/or YOTs may not be routinely aware of how many young people are currently subject to MAPPA.

The inconsistent understanding of MAPPA by YOT staff and the lack of awareness of YOT work encountered in some areas also suggested that training was an issue. The second recommendation made by Sutherland and Jones suggested that formalised risk training should include MAPPA alongside principles of assessment in general and specifically assessing risk of serious harm to others. Given YOTs' supervisory role and criminal justice remit, the authors also believed that variability in practice and lack of understanding could be ameliorated to some extent by the inclusion of YOTs as part of the Responsible Authority in each of the 42 MAPPA areas alongside the police, the probation service and the prison service. This would require a change in primary legislation, which there are no plans for, but the fact remains that YOTs have the same responsibilities as the probation service and it is thus an anomaly that they are not considered equal partners in this process.

A final recommendation was for a regulatory process to be implemented that would allow YOTs to report if young people were being excluded from the MAPPA process by additional local criteria that might jeopardise YOTs' ability to manage that case). Extending this, MAPPA coordinators should also have a recourse to highlighting if YOTs are not engaging with MAPPA locally, over and above existing mechanisms (for example via the YJB/PPU).

Conclusion

The recommendations noted above may go some way to addressing the issues reported by Sutherland and Jones. However, the focus of these recommendations is on the process and administration of YOTs and MAPPA. These were in part (mis?)guided by the belief that improvement and compliance with processes will enhance public protection outcomes. However, centring on processes misses much wider and arguably more important conceptual discussions about the interface of young people and YOT practitioners with a system designed for the control of dangerous adult offenders. This chapter has highlighted issues relating to YOTs (cosy thinking) and MAPP meetings (risk fatigue), which may make the practical engagement of one with the other more difficult. In doing so, occupational differences between YOTs and MAPPA are underlined. Primarily, this is in the way that YOTs have to adopt the language and views of MAPPA if they want to be taken seriously, in essence doing public protection 'on MAPPA terms' rather than 'on YOT terms'. Perhaps before further steps in this direction are taken, some thought should be given to MAPPA on YOT terms – where the risks presented are taken seriously, assessed properly and the differences between adults and young people are recognised and acknowledged.

Notes
[1] My thanks to Kerry Baker for her comments on this chapter.

[2] It should be noted that the information gathered for Lieb's work would have predated the introduction of the 2003/04 MAPPA guidance (Home Office, 2003, 2004).

References
Adams, J. (2003) 'Risk and morality: three framing devices', in R. Ericson and A. Doyle (eds) *Risk and Morality* (pp 87-104), London: University of Toronto Press.
Bailey, R., Knight, C. and Williams, B. (2007) 'The probation service as part of NOMS in England and Wales: fit for purpose?', in L. Gelsthorpe and R. Morgan (eds) *Handbook of Probation*, Cullompton: Willan.
Bennett, J. (2008) *The Social Costs of Dangerousness: Prison and the Dangerous Classes*, London: Centre for Crime and Justice Studies.

Bryan, T. and Doyle, P. (2003) 'Developing Multi-Agency Public Protection Arrangements', in A. Matravers (ed) *Sex Offenders in the Community: Managing and Reducing the Risks* (pp 189-206), Cullompton: Willan.

Burnett, R. and Appleton, C. (2004) *Joined-Up Youth Justice: Tackling Youth Crime in Partnership*, London: Russell House Publishing.

Burnett, R., Baker, K. and Roberts, C. (2007) 'Assessment, supervision and intervention: fundamental practice in probation', in L. Gelsthorpe and R. Morgan (eds) *Handbook of Probation*, Cullompton: Willan.

Campbell, E. (2004) 'Police narrativity in the risk society', *British Journal of Criminology*, vol 44, no 5, pp 695-714.

Eckersley, R.M. (2001) 'Losing the battle of the bulge: causes and consequences of increasing obesity', *Medical Journal of Australia*, vol 174, pp 590-2.

Ellis, T. and Boden, I. (2005) 'Is there a unifying professional culture in youth offending teams? A research note', British Society of Criminology 2004 (Volume 7) Conference Proceedings, available from www.britsoccrim.org/volume7/006.pdf

Ericson, R.V. and Haggerty, K.D. (1997) *Policing the Risk Society*, Oxford: Clarendon Press.

Haggerty, K. (2003) 'From risk to precaution: the rationalities of personal crime prevention', in R. Ericson and A. Doyle (eds) *Risk and Morality* (pp 193-214), London: University of Toronto Press.

Hayes, P. (2004) 'Debate on substance misuse: end-to-end provision within the criminal justice system – what are the gaps?', Comments made at the Youth Justice Annual Convention, London, available from www.yjb.gov.uk/

Home Office (2001) *Initial Guidance to the Police and Probation Services on Sections 67 & 68 of the Criminal Justice and Court Services Act 2000*, London: Home Office.

Home Office (2003) *MAPPA Guidance Version 1.0*, London: Home Office.

Home Office (2004) *MAPPA Guidance Version 1.2*, London: Home Office.

Kemshall, H. (2001) *Risk Assessment and Management of Known Sexual and Violent Offenders: A Review of Current Issues*, Police Research Series Paper No 140, London: Home Office.

Kemshall, H. (2002) 'Effective practice in probation: an example of 'advanced liberal' responsibilisation?', *Howard Journal*, vol 41, no 1, pp 41-58.

Kemshall, H., Mackenzie, G., Wood, J., Bailey, R. and Yates, J. (2005) *Strengthening Multi-Agency Public Protection Arrangements*, London: Home Office.

Lieb, R. (2003) 'Joined up worrying: the multi-agency public protection panels', in A. Matravers (ed) *Sex Offenders in the Community: Managing and Reducing the Risks* (pp 207-18), Cullompton: Willan Publishing.

McGuire, J. (1995) *What Works: Reducing Offending: Guidelines from Research and Practice*, Chichester and New York: Wiley.

Maguire, M., Kemshall, H., Noaks, L. and Wincup, E. (2001) *Risk Management of Sexual and Violent Offenders: The Work of Public Protection Panels*, Police Research Series No 139, London: Home Office.

Ministry of Justice (2007) *MAPPA Guidance Version 2.0*, National Offender Management Service, London: Ministry of Justice.

Moore, R., Gray, E., Roberts, C., Taylor, E. and Merrington, S. (2006) *Managing Persistent and Serious Offenders in the Community: Intensive Community Programmes in Theory and Practice*, Cullompton: Willan.

Morgan, R. and Newburn, T. (2007) 'Youth justice', in L. Gelsthorpe and R. Morgan (eds) *Handbook of Probation* (pp 292-321), Cullompton: Willan.

Munro, E. (1999) 'Common errors of reasoning in child protection work', *Child Abuse & Neglect*, vol 23, no 8, pp 745-58.

Nash, M. (2006) *Public Protection and the Criminal Justice Process*, Oxford: Oxford University Press.

Nash, M. (2007) 'Working with young people in a culture of public protection', in M. Blyth, E. Soloman and K. Baker (eds) *Young People and 'Risk'* (pp 85-95), Bristol: The Policy Press.

Nottinghamshire Social Services (1990) *Revised Joint Enquiry Report*, Nottingham: Nottingham Social Services, available from www.users.globalnet.co.uk/~dlheb/jetrepor.htm

Patton, M.Q. (1990) *Qualitative Evaluation and Research Methods* (2nd edition), Newbury Park, CA: Sage Publications.

Sutherland, A. and Jones, S. (2008) *MAPPA and Youth Justice: An Exploration of Youth Offending Team Engagement with Multi-Agency Public Protection Arrangements*, London: YJB.

Sutherland, A., Taylor, E., Gray, E., Merrington, S. and Roberts, C. (2007) *12-Month ISSP: Evaluation and Research findings*, London: YJB.

Wood, J. (2006) 'Profiling high-risk offenders: a review of 136 cases', *The Howard Journal*, vol 45, no 3, pp 307-20.

YJB (Youth Justice Board) (2006) *Multi-Agency Public Protection Arrangements: Guidance for Youth Offending Teams*, London: YJB.

YJB (2007) *Youth Justice Annual Workload Data 2006/07*, London: YJB.

YJB (2008) *Youth Justice: The Scaled Approach*, London: YJB.

4

Promoting public protection in youth justice: challenges for policy and practice

David Monk

Introduction

Tensions in our approach to children and young people who offend are by no means new and over the last 50 years or so these have been expressed in a variety of epithets, which, while headline grabbing, have not always been helpful. 'Social welfare' versus 'justice', 'deprived' versus 'depraved', 'deeds' versus 'needs' and 'care' versus 'control' are just a few examples of how this debate was framed in the post-war years, particularly the 1960s and 1970s. The tension remains today but the reformed youth justice system reflects a belief that different approaches can be used and that there is no one 'right' answer that excludes all others. Multi-agency Youth Offending Teams (YOTs) have to look both to criminal justice and welfare services to provide a cogent response to the complexities of youth offending. In addition, since 2007, the Youth Justice Board for England and Wales (YJB) has been jointly sponsored by the Ministry of Justice and the Department for Children, Schools and Families, reflecting the importance of this twin-track approach at the highest level.

Public protection in youth justice: key principles

Public protection is integral to youth justice practice

It is important that public protection in a youth justice context is seen as integral to wider approaches to working effectively with children and young people, rather than somehow separate and unconnected. *Managing Risk in the Community* (Wilkinson and Baker, 2005) encouraged managers and practitioners to distinguish clearly between risk (likelihood) of reoffending, risk of serious harm to others and vulnerability. While public protection is usually rightly equated most with preventing risk of serious harm to others, it must of course always be remembered that there should be a public protection pay-off through local youth justice providers' statutory responsibility to prevent offending by children and young people.[1] Moreover, young people themselves are part of the public (although perhaps not always seen as such) and therefore YOTs' attempts to work with others to minimise risks of vulnerability to young people themselves cannot sensibly be conceived of as unrelated to public protection.

The YJB has responsibility to advise ministers on National Standards for Youth Justice. These are currently being revised, with the intention that they are clearly described for youth justice staff as 'must dos' and that considerations of public protection are threaded throughout. A parallel piece of work has led to the development of new case management guidance for managers and practitioners (the 'how to do') in which public protection considerations are also reflected. Both are part of 'Youth Justice: The Scaled Approach' project (YJB, 2008a), which is being aligned with legislative change through the 2008 Criminal Justice and Immigration Act, which will bring about a new Youth Rehabilitation Order (YRO) for children and young people for implementation some time during 2009. As part of the same project, the YJB has recently published revised *Key Elements of Effective Practice* or KEEPs (YJB, 2008b), which seek to help practitioners and managers understand the 'what to do' in relation to the content of supervision for children and young people. All KEEPs have a relevance to public protection in that they describe effective practice in working with children and young people at risk of offending/reoffending. However, the revised KEEPs on *Assessment, Planning Interventions and Supervision* (APIS) and *Young People who Sexually Abuse* have a particular relevance in this context. In addition, the new KEEP on *Engaging Young People* provides guidance on how to engage young people to help them comply with their order and maintain good behaviour.

Public protection is the mirror image of safeguarding

There is a danger here that we see two largely separate populations of children and young people known to YOTs, the first at risk of committing serious harm to others and the second for whom safeguarding concerns may have been identified. The reality of course is more complex, since most people working in youth justice will confirm that they are very often the same children and young people.

The YJB oversees serious incident notifications from YOTs through the 'public protection' route (where the young person concerned has committed a very serious offence while under supervision or shortly afterwards) as well as the 'safeguarding' route (including death or attempted suicide of a young person while under supervision). This reveals some of the major underlying complexities in this area, including the dangers of drawing too rigid a distinction between public protection on the one hand and safeguarding on the other. Take, for example, the case of a young man under YOT supervision who dies at the wheel of a car while driving his friends the wrong way down a motorway, killing his friends who are passengers, as well as an adult driving the car with which he collided. The young man's behaviour is both dangerous to himself (safeguarding) but also to others (public protection). Most importantly of all, it represents a tragedy for all concerned, regardless of how it is conceived by the professionals involved.

The duality of the youth justice approach to public protection and safeguarding is reflected clearly by YOTs' roles and responsibilities not only in relation to Multi-Agency Public Protection Arrangements (MAPPA) (YJB, 2006a) but also Local Safeguarding Children Boards (LSCBs) as set out in the 2004 Children Act. It is important to note that while responsibility for complying with the duty to promote the safeguarding and welfare of children and young people may sit particularly heavily on YOTs' shoulders given their day-to-day work with children and young people, it is in fact a duty that is also shared under the same legislation with the police, the probation service and the prison service as MAPPA Responsible Authorities.

Public protection is a shared responsibility

The YJB is not an employer of staff delivering services to children and young people and therefore there is not a simple 'command-and-control' mechanism in play. However, the YJB shares responsibility for 'getting it right' with local services through establishing the framework – standards, guidance and workforce development – that informs practice and facilitates improvement in the delivery of services.

Similarly, the concept of shared responsibility between practitioners and managers in youth justice is critically important. HM Inspectorate of Probation's (HMIP) joint inspection of YOTs suggests that, while managers are increasingly likely to know about medium-/high-risk cases on a YOT's caseload, they are still often not involved in active managerial oversight of such cases. By way of illustration, referral of medium-/high-risk-of-harm cases to managers increased from 61% in phase one of the inspections (September 2003 to September 2004) to 71% in phase two (September 2004 to July 2005) and to 85% in phase three (July 2005 to January 2007) (HMIP, 2007). However, the HMIP data indicate more modest movement in terms of managerial oversight, with this having increased from 41% in phase one to 48% in phase three. This would appear to suggest that this is a tougher nut to crack and one from which YOTs might learn from adult correctional services.

Finally, there is a need for shared responsibility between YOTs as service delivery entities (including both managers and practitioners) on the one hand and YOT management boards on the other. Youth Offending Team management boards provide crucial strategic oversight of local service delivery and as such have key responsibilities in relation to public protection in local YOTs. *Sustaining the Success* (YJB, 2004) set out the overarching governance framework for YOTs in the context of their unique role in straddling key policy areas in both criminal justice and children's services. It is intended that this will be revised in the future to take account of the rapidly changing external environment in which YOTs are operating, most notably changes in the performance landscape and further development of integrated working at a local level.

Children are not 'mini adults'

The assessment process is crucial to identifying public protection issues and putting in place a plan for managing these (see Kemshall and Wood, this volume). Assessment generally is a complex task, but never more so with children and young people whose behaviour can change quickly (as we may all testify if memory serves us well!). Additionally, young people's level of risk of future serious harm will very often not be indicated by the number or nature of previous convictions, but by behaviour at school, in the streets or at home. Core *Asset* documentation (through the 'Indicators of Serious Harm' section) prompts a full Risk of Serious Harm Assessment (ROSH) to be undertaken in particular circumstances. These include the young person having been convicted of serious specified offences or being sentenced at Crown Court for a specified offence, or when a youth court has specifically requested that a YOT should contribute to the court's assessment of dangerousness to determine whether the case should be committed to Crown Court (YJB, 2006b). However, *Asset* also provides an opportunity to identify those behaviours that may be indicative of future risk of serious harm, through questions relating to a range of disconcerting or disturbing behaviour by the young person, for example cruelty to animals.

Youth justice practitioners are not 'tick box' technicians

There is major value in requiring youth justice practitioners to operate within defined structures and parameters in order to assist decision making and *Asset* is one such example. Indeed, the YJB is presently considering introducing further structure to the offence analysis section of the Core *Asset* profile as completion of this section is traditionally weak and over-dependent on description rather than analysis. However, this is not the whole story since a good *Asset* requires effective engagement with the young person, along with a high level of assessment skills in order to know which risk factors are present, how to evidence them and how to link assessed need with subsequent intervention. Baker (2007) also suggests that there are some critical questions that need to be considered when trying to analyse information collected in a particular case; for instance about the reliability of evidence, links between disparate pieces of information and what possible alternative hypotheses need to be considered.

The YJB's National Qualifications Framework (NQF) has similarly sought to provide local staff with a structure in which to understand effective practice with children and young people, while not prescribing the detail of practice from the centre. The YJB is working to align the NQF with broader workforce developments in England and Wales and is in the process of setting out a new youth justice workforce strategic framework for the period 2008-11 (YJB, 2008c). This plans to bring about an incremental transfer to local youth justice providers of the core responsibility for ensuring that local staff are well trained and competent to deliver high-quality youth justice services. Central to these plans is a major expansion of web-based learning, which retains key concepts such as the reflective practitioner, while enabling much greater flexibility in terms of access to materials.

Developing public protection in youth justice through working with others

The YJB works closely with a range of partners to support youth justice policy and practice developments in relation to public protection, including the Public Protection Unit (PPU) of the National Offender Management Service (NOMS), the Parole Board for England and Wales and, of course, YOTs themselves.

NOMS PPU

The YJB has contributed to the NOMS Public Protection Board and uses this as an opportunity to understand the latest thinking in relation to developments in the adult criminal justice system and consider their potential applicability to young people. At the same time, it is important to keep in mind some of the key differences between adults and young people, as well as the very different arrangements in place at a local level for the delivery of youth justice services.

The role of YOTs in MAPPA has also been a focus for attention. One of the early concerns voiced by many YOTs in relation to MAPPA has been that, despite their inclusion as an agency with a 'duty to cooperate' through the 2003 Criminal Justice Act, arrangements on the ground have generally remained adult focused. This is in part a product of the fact that YOTs took their place at the MAPPA table some time after the police and the probation service had established closer working relationships. Also, YOTs' status as a 'duty to cooperate' agency is unique among other such agencies in that, among these, only YOTs have responsibilities for the statutory supervision of individuals who have offended. This does not necessarily add up to an argument for a change of legislation to make YOTs part of Responsible Authorities, but is noteworthy nevertheless. Finally, the number of young people subject to the MAPPA process is relatively small compared with the adult population, and there is therefore a strong but unwarranted tendency for them to be accorded a lower priority (see Sutherland, this volume).

Joint work with the PPU has recently focused on contributing to revised national MAPPA guidance in which the place of YOTs in the process is clearer and more prominent than before (Ministry of Justice, 2007). This has included the development of a specific annex to the main guidance, which focuses exclusively on the issues presented by children and young people being considered in a MAPPA context. This focuses particularly on issues such as the identification of appropriate cases, thresholds for referral, information sharing, management and disclosure.

Work has also been completed between the YJB and the PPU to develop a standardised set of documentation for use by YOTs in relation to children, young people and the MAPPA process. This includes a mechanism for YOT notification of category 1 and 2 cases to local MAPPA coordinators where the YOT has assessed level 1 supervision to be appropriate, and for referral to MAPPA of category 1-3 cases where active multi-agency involvement (level 2 or 3) is sought. The referral form encapsulates the critical issues relating to the particular needs of young people and how future risk of serious harm may be reflected in behaviours outside of the criminal justice process. Youth Offending Teams and local MAPPA coordinators have often not agreed in the past on thresholds for referral of a young person to the MAPPA process and it is anticipated that this will assist in enhancing common understanding of the particular ways in which future risk of serious harm may be manifested in young people. Standard documentation and consistent expectations on both sides in relation to young people should go a long way towards resolving the difficulties highlighted by the research commissioned by the YJB (Sutherland and Jones, 2008). There is an intention to build on this by ensuring the contribution of a youth justice perspective at regular conferences held by the PPU, as well as input into national training for MAPPA chairs. However, nothing can substitute for the development of strong and healthy relationships at a local level between YOTs and MAPPA coordinators and this should be a priority for all those concerned, in order that different perspectives are shared and mutual understanding developed.

The YJB is currently revising its own bespoke MAPPA guidance for YOTs and the secure estate (YJB, forthcoming) in the light of these broader national developments. Revised guidance on serious incident reporting procedures (YJB, 2007a) also connects with broader MAPPA processes, requiring the YOT Local Management Report (LMR) following the commission of a very serious offence to be made available to the MAPPA coordinator. These reports will become important in the broader environment, as MAPPA implement new requirements for Serious Case Reviews.

Parole Board for England and Wales

The YJB has also embarked on a joint programme of work with the Parole Board in view of the small but increasing number of children and young people serving custodial sentences for which release is dependent on a decision by the Parole Board, as a result of the public protection sentences introduced by the 2003 Criminal Justice Act (Sections 226 and 228). Prior to this, release and recall arrangements only applied to young people sentenced under Sections 90 and 91 of the 2000 Powers of Criminal Courts (Sentencing) Act and in practice most young people were transferred to adult services prior to their release. The provisions of the 2003 Criminal Justice Act therefore provided both an opportunity as well as a necessity for YOTs to 'up their game' in relation to this group of young people who have often committed the most serious and high-profile offences.

The YJB has produced guidance on YOTs' role in the early release and recall of young people subject to such sentences, in consultation with the Parole Board and other key stakeholders (YJB, 2007b). The key purpose of the guidance is to provide YOTs with the means to ensure that local practice contributes to adequate public protection in relation to young people who have committed the most serious and high-profile offences; that victims are consulted where appropriate; and that young people subject to the new provisions are released at the earliest possible opportunity, consistent with the risk they pose. Also underpinning the guidance are expectations that effective risk management plans should be in place; that breaches of licence conditions and increases in risk of serious harm should be dealt with effectively and speedily by YOTs; and that YOTs should be able to demonstrate defensible decision making throughout the process.

There are significant issues to be faced in relation to the important matter of how young people are provided with the opportunity to demonstrate a reduction in 'risk' over the course of the custodial part of the sentence, in order to inform the decision-making process by the Parole Board. It has been suggested that one way to demonstrate a reduction in risk would be for young people to show that they have completed an offending behaviour programme. However, the YJB has deliberately chosen not to go down the road of accredited programmes in the same way as the adult sector, instead requiring providers to review their provision against the key criteria set out in KEEPs. One of these criteria is to ensure that they first determine whether someone is at high likelihood of reoffending before deciding whether they are suitable for a programme. The concern in accrediting programmes is that they may be considered 'effective' regardless of who undertakes them. The YJB approach to effective practice means that secure establishments dealing with children and young people provide a range of interventions to address offending behaviour, rather than a uniform approach. In any event, it is clear that completion of a programme by the child or young person would not itself satisfy the Parole Board's considerations in relation to reduction of likelihood of further offending and/or risk of serious harm.

Behaviour in custody is likely to be one facet of Parole Board decision making in relation to suitability for release. However, the limitations of this approach may be more evident for children and young people than for adults, and a poor proxy for future behaviour on the outside. The Parole Board will also be interested to know whether the young person has developed insight into their offending behaviour. This too may pose particular difficulties for children and young people who may be less able to articulate their thoughts than adults and have less experience of 'playing the system'.

An indication that the young person has matured in terms of attitude and motivation is critically important to considerations of the Parole Board, and in this respect children and young people should be at an advantage, in that most do mature and develop improved cognitive skills with age. However, the challenge here is how to provide young people with an opportunity to have such positive change recorded systematically and in a way that justifies such conclusions being drawn as a basis for decision making. In addition to the YJB's ongoing programme of *Asset* development, there are plans to give future consideration to the value of other measures (including perhaps psychometric testing) that could help to give a reliable indication of attitudinal change over time. Finally, the Parole Board will be seeking robust but realistic release plans. This can raise particular complexities in that young people generally have fewer options for relocation or resettlement than adults and are particularly dependent on professionals to provide appropriate services and support in this process. The challenge for the YJB and YOTs is to drive up practice in this area, while encouraging an appreciation by the Parole Board of some of the particular issues faced by young people in this respect.

The Parole Board's decision to extend the right to automatic oral hearings for all juvenile cases as soon as they come before the Board (Parole Board, 2008) has been warmly welcomed by the YJB. This followed the Howard League for Penal Reform (2007) review of the parole process for children in *Parole 4 Kids*. The Parole Board had previously been criticised by the courts over the case of 15-year-old 'K', for allowing his case to be decided without ensuring that he had sufficient advice and help available to him. This represents a change from the previous position where oral hearings for determinate sentence juveniles were only offered in exceptional circumstances and means that all juveniles will get a chance to be present at their hearing, have their say in person and ensure that they are legally represented. This raises new challenges for YOTs in understanding the rules of engagement in the hitherto unfamiliar forum of oral hearings, and probation secondees to YOTs should be well placed to assist this process. It also raises challenges for the Parole Board in explaining to all participants the process and purpose of such hearings in order to maximise their effectiveness and inclusiveness.

Further progress in relation to meeting the needs of children and young people subject to the parole process will need to be worked through, including consideration of the advantages of children's cases being considered by Parole Board members with specialist knowledge in this area. This would mirror specialist arrangements for dealing with children elsewhere in the criminal justice system, for example through YOTs and, of course, youth courts. Additionally, arrangements need to be in place for this group to ensure that their cases are considered by MAPPA prior to eligibility for release, in order that risk management plans are in place to inform the Parole Board's considerations.

YOTs

Public protection policies

An audit of YOT public protection policies commissioned by the YJB provided valuable insight into their progress in developing organisational policies focusing specifically on those children and young people at risk of committing serious harm to others (Social Information Systems, 2007).[2] In total, 88 YOTs (56% of the total) provided their policy. Overall, there was no one single example that could be held up as a template for what such a policy should look like, with some of the fuller policies having significant gaps while other briefer policies had excellent sections. Most YOTs defined the core *Asset* profile as the start point of the process, made specific reference to the requirement to undertake a ROSH assessment when any one indicator of significant harm to others was identified in the core *Asset*, and defined ongoing case management and review arrangements. However, the definitions of roles and responsibilities for the core processes of risk management were not always clearly detailed, with indicative timescales to discharge such processes varying substantially between YOTs. For example, there were different expectations in relation to the frequency with which high- and very high-risk cases should be reviewed; some policies required that such cases should be reviewed weekly, whereas others required only monthly reviews.

Overall, attention was shown to the MAPPA agenda in the majority of policies submitted, although it was of concern that eight of the policies (9%) made no reference to MAPPA at all. In many of those that did, there was a lack of distinction between MAPPA categories and levels, and also a lack of clarity with regard to the role of the ROSH form in triggering referral to MAPPA. Finally, YOTs' considerations of serious harm issues tended to be stronger at the earlier stages of the process of engagement with children and weaker during later stages such as the interface between custody and community or transition to adult services for young people reaching the age of 18.

The YJB has since worked with YOTs through a series of regional workshops and an extensive consultation process with external stakeholders, for example HMIP, to develop an exemplar public protection policy for use by YOTs against which to assess their practice and plan improvements. This will better enable YOTs to set out their policy in relation to public protection, including the review cycle and implementation procedures, and ensure that all YOT staff understand and apply the policy in their work. The exemplar clarifies key areas of responsibility for aspects of public protection policy and practice, and should support and enable YOT management boards, managers and staff to understand their respective roles in this area of work. Consideration is also given to the identification of key interfaces with other existing guidance and YOT policy areas as well as with other agencies sharing a responsibility for protecting the public.

The YJB's revised National Standards for Youth Justice and case management guidance (expected to be published during 2009 to coincide with the introduction of the YRO) will both reinforce the importance of YOTs' attention to delivering on the public protection agenda in the context of local public protection policies and YOTs' role in the MAPPA process. The new youth justice planning framework for YOTs in England contains key sections that require self-assessment by the YOT and validation by the YJB of YOTs' capacity and capability to deliver in relation to the assessment and management of risk of serious harm specifically, as well in relation to the prevention and reduction of reoffending by children and young people more generally.

Gangs and serious group offending

High-profile cases of young people involved in gangs and serious group offending have generated significant challenges for public protection and MAPPA. For example, some young people who have committed very serious offences in gangs may have had no previous involvement in the youth justice system and their motivation for involvement may be much more linked with peer influence than other types of offending. Research published by the YJB has also highlighted a need for more focused work in this area (Young et al, 2007).

A dedicated post at the YJB was created in 2007 in order to work collaboratively with YOTs as well as secure providers in order to pull together the strands affecting this emerging issue and develop a strategy to enable YOTs to work more effectively in this field. This includes the development of guidance around identification, screening and assessment, data recording and management, as well as identifying and showcasing innovative programmes of prevention and intervention. Further planned developments of *Asset* will add questions to the neighbourhood and lifestyle sections in relation to gangs and serious group offending to assist practitioners and managers to include this as an integral part of their assessment. Work is in hand to link this agenda with safeguarding in general and the role of LSCBs in particular. In this context, the YJB has contributed to work being undertaken by the London Safeguarding Children Board on the development of procedures for safeguarding children affected by gang activity.[3]

Quality of assessment

Youth Offending Teams have made substantial improvements in the completion of *Asset* documentation over the last few years and the challenge is now to improve the quality of assessments, for example the range of evidence provided, and the link between the risk factors highlighted in the assessment process and the intervention delivered. Major developments in relation to the electronic exchange of information between YOTs and secure facilities have both highlighted the challenge in relation to assessments completed on children and young people being made the subject of Detention and Training Orders (DTOs) as well as provided opportunities for improvement activities through additional funding.

The particular challenge of delivering effective public protection with children and young people in a youth justice context has already been noted. Nevertheless, it is clear that YOTs are not yet using the relevant section of the *Asset* core profile ('Indicators of Serious Harm') or the full ROSH assessment to maximum effect, with ROSHs not always completed as required (Baker, 2007). This system has been designed to help YOTs navigate the particular challenge of managing serious harm in a youth justice context. There may be a concern among some YOT practitioners about the dangers of 'labelling' young people through this process. However, the completion of a full ROSH assessment does ensure that a thorough and documented risk assessment is undertaken and, crucially, that appropriate risk management plans can be put in place in the event that an assessment of high or very high risk is reached. *Asset* documentation in general and in relation to assessment of serious harm in particular is under regular review by the YJB and further changes are planned in order to improve its usefulness in this regard.

Assessment and management of risk of serious harm and the 'scaled' approach

Youth Justice: The Scaled Approach (YJB, 2008a) has at its core the intention to move away from a 'one-size-fits-all' approach to the supervision of children and young people in the community to the provision of differential intervention levels according to the risk and needs of young people. This represents the most fundamental reworking of the practice framework since YOTs were first established a decade ago and such an approach depends critically on sustainable improvements to the assessment process being achieved. The approach has been developed incrementally by the YJB, working closely with four pilot YOTs, as well as a range of stakeholders through an extensive consultation process (Morgan Harris Burrows, forthcoming).

Intervention levels will be driven by an assessment of the likelihood of reoffending as well as the risk of serious harm to others being committed, with the highest of one 'trumping' the other in order to ensure that adequate intervention levels are in place for the young person concerned. Required levels of contact will be embedded in revised National Standards for Youth Justice as well as case management guidance for managers and practitioners. This approach will require substantial change for YOTs in terms of practice, management and strategic oversight and is expected to achieve higher levels of intervention for those young people who pose a high risk of serious harm and therefore the greatest challenge in terms of public protection. This shift in practice is likely to mean a greater synergy between local YOTs and MAPPA in terms of their priorities and the availability of higher levels of YOT intervention to support those cases that are referred to MAPPA for level 2 or 3 supervision.

Conclusion

The greatest challenge for policy and practice in relation to promoting public protection in youth justice is that children and young people are by their nature still developing. Given their age, there is much less 'solid' antecedent information to go on than with adults and that which does exist can be difficult to find and attach a meaning to. Good progress has been made in developing public protection in this context and has been achieved through work with key partners such as NOMS to strengthen the links between YOTs and MAPPA as well as the Parole Board for England and Wales. Major work has been undertaken with YOTs in relation to the development of local public protection policies and is continuing in relation to group offending and gangs, as well as the 'scaled approach' to youth justice. Further progress will depend on improvements to YOT practice in relation to assessment and management of those young people at risk of committing serious harm to others. This will be assisted by the move to differential levels of intervention for children and young people in the youth justice system, supported by revised National Standards for Youth Justice, a full range of guidance informed by the latest evidence and a new legislative framework. Further improvements in public protection policy and practice will depend on working closely with partners and stakeholders to enhance still further YOTs' role in MAPPA. Most important of all, we should always remember that we cannot sensibly think about public protection in youth justice without also considering the need to safeguard the child or young person.

Notes

[1] As required by the 1998 Crime and Disorder Act.

[2] This followed the publication of *Managing Risk in the Community* (Wilkinson and Baker, 2005), which emphasised the importance of such policies being developed at a local level.

[3] See www.londonscb.gov.uk/gangs/

References

Baker, K. (2007) 'Risk assessment in practice: systems and practitioner judgement', in M. Blyth, E. Solomon and K. Baker (eds) *Young People and 'Risk'* (pp 25-38), Bristol: The Policy Press.

HMIP (Her Majesty's Inspectorate of Probation) (2007) *Joint Inspection of Youth Offending Teams Annual Report 2006/07*, London: HMIP.

Howard League for Penal Reform (2007) *Parole 4 Kids: A Review of the Parole Process for Children in England and Wales*, London: Howard League for Penal Reform.

Ministry of Justice (2007) *MAPPA Guidance Version 2.0*, National Offender Management Service, London: Ministry of Justice.

Morgan Harris Burrows (forthcoming) *Process Evaluation of the Pilot of a Risk-Based Approach to Interventions*, London: YJB.

Parole Board (2008) *Parole Board Response to Howard League Review of the Parole Process for Children*, www.paroleboard.gov.uk/news/response_to_howard_league_re view/

Social Information Systems (2007) *Risk Management Policies of Youth Offending Teams: Evaluation Overview*, London: YJB, www.yjb.gov.uk/publications

Sutherland, A. and Jones, S. (2008) *MAPPA and Youth Justice: An Exploration of Youth Offending Team Engagement with Multi-Agency Public Protection Arrangements*, London: YJB.

Wilkinson, B. and Baker, K. (2005) *Managing Risk in the Community* (1st edition), London: YJB.

YJB (Youth Justice Board) (2004) *Sustaining the Success*, London: YJB.

YJB (2006a) *Multi-Agency Public Protection Arrangements: Guidance for Youth Offending Teams*, London: YJB, www.yjb.gov.uk /publications

YJB (2006b) *Asset: An Assessment Framework for Young People Involved in the Youth Justice System*, London: YJB.

YJB (2007a) *Serious Incidents: Guidance on Serious Incident Reporting Procedures*, London: YJB.

YJB (2007b) *Release and Recall: Guidance for Youth Offending Teams*, London: YJB.

YJB (2008a) *Youth Justice: The Scaled Approach*, London: YJB.

YJB (2008b) *Key Elements of Effective Practice*, London: YJB.

YJB (2008c) *Workforce Development Strategy: A Strategic Framework 2008-11*, London: YJB.

YJB (forthcoming: 2009) *MAPPA Guidance for YOTs* (2nd edition), London: YJB.

Young, T., Fitzgerald, M., Hallsworth, S. and Joseph, I. (2007) *Groups, Gangs and Weapons*, London: YJB.

Part Two
Risk management through MAPPA: the right approach for young people?

5

Young people, serious offending and managing risk: a Scottish perspective

Fergus McNeill

Introduction

This chapter explores some of the issues surrounding the assessment and management of young people who have been involved in serious offending in Scotland. It begins by outlining how Multi-Agency Public Protection Arrangements (MAPPA) have been set up in Scotland and identifies some of the practical challenges and issues that have arisen in the early implementation of these arrangements. The second section of the chapter briefly reviews some of the findings of a recent literature review on the risk assessment and risk management of children and young people engaging in offending behaviours. The review was commissioned by the Risk Management Authority and undertaken by staff of the Scottish Centre for Crime and Justice Research (Burman et al, 2008). The final, and most speculative, section of the chapter considers some wider questions about the tensions between practice models based on risk and those concerned with the promotion of 'good lives' – particularly in terms of how these debates relate to children and young people.

MAPPA in Scotland: sounds familiar?

MAPPA in Scotland have a much shorter history than those in England and Wales. The arrangements were introduced through Sections 10 and 11 of the 2005 Management of Offenders (Scotland) Act and, at the time of writing, they apply only to adult offenders (meaning those aged 16 and over). Essentially, as in England and Wales, the legislation requires a number of 'Responsible Authorities' – the police, the Scottish Prison Service, health boards and local authorities – to put in place joint arrangements for the assessment and management of risks posed by certain categories of offenders. It is important to note that in Scotland there is no separate probation service and probation functions continue to be undertaken by criminal justice social workers (CJSWs) within local authorities (McNeill and Whyte, 2007). However, the Responsible Authority in MAPPA is not the social work department, but rather the local authority as a whole. The legislation also allows the Scottish

Parliament to specify 'duty to cooperate' agencies who, as the name suggests, must cooperate with the Responsible Authorities in establishing and implementing the arrangements; these include but are not limited to housing providers, relevant voluntary organisations and SERCO (the company responsible for the electronic monitoring of offenders in Scotland).

Again as in England and Wales, there are three categories of offenders and three levels of risk management. The three categories are registered sex offenders, serious violent offenders (meaning those convicted under solemn procedures in the Sheriff Solemn or High Court) and other convicted offenders who are deemed to pose a risk of serious harm (which may include some mentally disordered offenders). The three levels are:

- level 1: 'ordinary risk management' (where low-to-medium risk offenders can be safely managed by one agency);
- level 2: 'interagency risk management' (where medium-to-high risk offenders require inter-agency measures to be put in place);
- level 3: Multi-Agency Public Protection Panel (MAPPP) cases (where the 'critical few' very high-risk or 'notorious' offenders require the full panoply of MAPPA coordination).

I noted above that in law these arrangements apply only to adult offenders, but of course (as civil servants have pointed out) there is no technical reason why MAPPA meetings should not be informally extended to consider children and young people in respect of whom significant concern exists.

Scottish practitioners charged with the responsibility of implementing MAPPA have noted a number of early challenges.[1] First, it has not always been easy for those involved in risk assessment to get an accurate story of the offence and of the offending history. It may surprise readers from other jurisdictions to find that Scottish Social Enquiry Report writers do not have routine access to police reports and witness statements; for reasons that remain somewhat unclear, the Crown Office in Scotland has always been reticent about this kind of access. While the increased level of police–CJSW cooperation that MAPPA have required has begun to address this issue, it may take some time for information sharing to become the norm rather than the exception. Second, and the point is related, while there have been rapid developments in Scotland around the assessment of risk in connection with those who have committed sex offences, the assessment of risk in connection with violent offending is much less well developed. This is an area that the Risk Management Authority in Scotland is currently seeking to address, but those involved in MAPPA continue to have some concerns both about available risk assessment instruments and about the levels of resourcing that will be required when violent offenders become part of the MAPPA arrangements during the next stage of implementation.[2] Third, in establishing MAPPA, CJSWs have faced new challenges in developing communication and joint planning with colleagues in the health service, with the courts and with the Parole Board; communication with the Parole Board around the insertion of appropriate conditions in release licences is a major issue.

Beyond these practical concerns, MAPPA in Scotland raise wider issues – just as they do in England and Wales (see Kemshall, this volume). On the positive side, there is widespread support for the development of a consistent approach across Scotland; an aspiration that is particularly challenging given the absence of a national probation service and some evidence of disparate practices in different areas. Similarly, practitioners and policy makers share a common concern to see the development of effective and efficient risk management arrangements that are parsimonious; that is, which manage offenders at the lowest and least intrusive level that is consistent with public safety. That said, there are a number of legal and moral concerns about the sustainability of this parsimony in the context of the obvious political sensitivities about risk at the local and national levels. And indeed within the MAPPA guidance itself (available online at www.scotland.gov.uk/Publications/2008/04/18144823/53) – specifically around the management of 'notorious' offenders – there is more than a hint of preoccupation with 'reputational risk' to national and local government, rather than risk to the public per se. Of course, this preoccupation itself generates the risk that far from favouring parsimonious interventions in the lives of offenders that respect their rights, MAPPA may contribute significantly to the net-widening and mesh-thinning through which the late-modern state increases its carceral reach (Cohen, 1985), partly as a means of offsetting its increasing economic impotence in the face of globalisation, and the challenges to its legitimacy thus created (Bauman, 2000; Garland, 2001; McCulloch and McNeill, 2007). That MAPPA function as an administrative (and at best *quasi*-legal) process with no obvious right of appeal or review is concerning, especially given that, under the twin pressures of a risk-averse society and its blame culture, there are anecdotal reports of practitioners in England and Wales reverting to 'constructive breach' or 'pre-emptive enforcement'; that is, in cases where released offenders pose very serious concerns, the temptation is to load licences with untenable conditions in order to precipitate breach and recall to custody. In this context, the informal extension of MAPPA to children and young people, despite some obvious potential benefits, raises further concerns.

The Scottish review

Against this backdrop, the Risk Management Authority's[3] decision to commission a literature review on the risk assessment and management of children and young people involved in serious offending was a welcome and timely development; the decision followed a series of consultations that identified the need for work in this area.

The resulting study (Burman et al, 2008) contained two elements. The first was a literature review focused on processes, strategies, tools and techniques for risk assessment and management. It drew mainly on the research literature from the

UK, the US and Canada, but was necessarily selective rather than exhaustive. The second aspect of the study was a focused survey of current practice in the assessment and management of children and young people at risk of harm and reoffending in Scotland. The survey was conducted mainly by telephone interview and was designed to complement the literature review by sharpening its focus on those issues relevant to the Scottish context. Twenty-one telephone interviews were conducted, primarily with practitioners involved in risk assessment and management. Full details of the methodology of the study are provided in the final report of the study (Burman et al, 2008).

Although the Scottish study does provide a useful account of the development, strengths and limitations of risk assessment in general, and of risk assessment in relation to violent and sexual offending by children and young people in particular, these issues are not the focus of this chapter. More pertinent here are Burman et al's (2008) conclusions from their review of the literature on risk *management* in relation to children and young people.

The review notes that the literature suggests a growing tendency across many jurisdictions to deploy a range of interventions that seek to address both the needs of the young person *and* the protection of the public. This entails a holistic approach that targets the young person's overall situation, including their personal and social relationships. There is a high degree of consensus in the literature that a challenge exists in ensuring that strategies for intervention and risk management are properly developed from risk assessment. To some extent, this is related to the fact that, although there has been a rapid development of a large pool of research, this has been vastly outpaced by political and public interest in serious offending by young people and children. Despite the expanding knowledge base, the political context of risk management has sometimes led to investment in programmes, interventions and strategies despite minimal, weak or flawed evidence of their effectiveness. In effect, the review suggests that while the evidence base for work with children and young people who engage in sexually harmful behaviour has improved, and there is also an emerging body of research on effective interventions for young people who engage in violent behaviours, there are still some significant limitations and gaps in the literature.

Burman et al (2008) note that there is a preference in the UK and elsewhere for programmes informed by cognitive behavioural therapy (CBT) models. For example, England and Wales have adopted this approach in probation and youth justice (see Burnett and Roberts, 2004), and the Youth Justice Board (YJB) included a significant evaluation component alongside investment in CBT programmes for a variety of offending types such as persistent offending and sexually aggressive behaviour. In North America and in some places in the UK, multi-systemic therapy (MST) has also gained favour; MST formalises common treatment ideas flowing from developmental and systemic perspectives. Burman et al (2008) suggest that a number of well-designed studies have provided considerable evidence of its success. Family systems approaches are found to be more frequently used in the UK when working with young people who sexually abuse; these approaches have demonstrated significant levels of effectiveness, for example in reducing long-term rates of reoffending and imprisonment. In general, there is clear evidence that well-structured community-based alternatives to secure confinement for addressing even young people's serious offending are at least as effective in reducing reoffending as institutional or custodial measures.

Multi-agency working is a typical recommendation of the research on management of young people's offending risks, although (as we will see below) there are considerable conceptual and practical challenges to its effective implementation. As well as strong relationships between professionals and agencies, the literature suggests that establishing a strong, secure relationship between the young person and the worker is a prerequisite of successful intervention. The importance of appropriate training on the use of risk assessment tools and on risk management is also underlined in several studies.

Turning to Burman et al's (2008) survey of Scottish practice, they found that referrals for risk assessments come from a wide variety of sources at varying stages in a young person's life and thus require contact with several agencies in order to gather the requisite information and complete the process fully. The most commonly cited aims of risk assessment were to identify the risk of harm, to explore reasons for offending, to identify wider needs in a young person's life and to develop appropriate action plans as a result. The major aim of risk assessment was related more to welfare and need than to 'justice', although practitioners acknowledged that this could create tensions with other agencies.

Quality assurance was gained through the accountability required in a multi-agency context, as well as through supervision, auditing of outputs and outcomes, and reviews of action plans. While some agencies used aggregated data from individual risk assessments to inform future policy and practice, this was not done on a systematic basis.

The two main tools used for risk assessment were the Youth Level of Service/Case Management Inventory (YLS/CMI) and *Asset*, both of which were to varying degrees seen as appropriate for young people, although not necessarily for young women or those with problematic sexual behaviours. Practitioners were optimistic that risk assessment tools complement professional judgement even though there was an acknowledgement that different agencies had different professional interpretations of risk and how to address it. Inter-agency collaboration was seen as crucial in risk assessment and management and there was optimism that it was working well in Scotland. Apart from the issue of problematic sexual behaviour, respondents cited a plethora of agencies and programmes that aided the process of working with vulnerable young people.

In respect of high-risk cases, multi-agency collaboration was again deemed both essential and constructive, allowing not only for accountability and defensible decision making but also better outcomes for young people. Tensions cited by interviewees related to the dichotomy of welfare versus justice orientations – not least for young people at the interface between the Children's Hearings[4] and criminal justice systems. In this regard, thresholds of risk varied between agencies, depending on their respective constituencies, remits and cultures.

Overall, what Burman et al's (2008) review reveals is that although risk assessment and risk management are rapidly developing fields of knowledge, weaknesses in the evidence base remain, and that these weaknesses when coupled with the political sensitivities generated in the pursuit of public protection produce a complex and contested site of practice. Moreover, this contested site of practice is one in which different personal, organisational and cultural perspectives on and tolerances of risk overlap, interact and, often, conflict. Although it is not a point that Burman et al (2008) make directly, the overview that they present suggests that risk assessment and management, although often clothed in technical and even scientific language, are inescapably *moral* and *social* practices that are profoundly influenced and shaped by their cultural and political contexts.

Risk, good lives and getting it right

Recognition of the significance of the cultural and political contexts of risk is hardly novel or surprising, but it does invite us to ask fundamental but often neglected questions about the foundations of risk assessment and risk management – rather than the more frequently addressed questions (in practice at least) around validity and reliability. Thus, commentators have raised concerns about due process, justice and proportionality (Rose, 1998; Hudson, 2001, 2003); moral and political dimensions of risk (Stenson and Sullivan, 2001; Gray et al, 2002; Ericson and Doyle, 2003); gender, racial and culture discrimination (Hannah-Moffat and Shaw, 2001); the targeting of marginalised populations and the redistribution of resources based on risk profiles (Rose, 1998; O'Malley, 1999; Silver and Miller, 2002); and the sometimes tenuous relationships between risk and rehabilitation or 'what works' initiatives (Kemshall, 1998; Robinson, 1999, 2002; Hannah-Moffat, 2005).

However, it is also necessary to ask conceptual questions about the ways that we think about and engage with 'risk'. For example, does it really make sense to conceptualise and discuss risk as an attribute of individuals? In this vein, Kemshall (2003) has described the unarticulated but important epistemological assumptions underlying the distinction between what is called 'artefact risk' (seeing risk as a product of relatively stable traits and characteristics) and 'constructivist risk' (seeing risk as a social construct, contingent on all sorts of social contexts and processes). A recent and detailed empirical study of young people's developmental pathways, carried out within the Economic and Social Research Council-funded 'Pathways Into and Out of Crime for Young People' network, suggests that the import and meaning of risk factors is indeed highly context- and case-specific (see Boeck et al, 2006). This resonates with Laub and Sampson's (2003) compelling arguments against the risk factor paradigm. In their retrospective analysis of the lives of 70-year-old men (on whom relevant data has been collected since their childhoods), they found that men who shared similar risk profiles as children had markedly different life trajectories and that these differences were not in any sense predictable.

Of course, such perspectives are compatible with other theoretical perspectives that are frequently advanced in working with children and young people. Thus, for example, within social work, there is a long tradition of employing developmental perspectives and ecological approaches (Aldgate, 2007) in working with children and families. These perspectives assert the importance of understanding human characteristics and behaviours within their social and developmental contexts, of recognising and supporting the potential for human development, of analysing the significance of interactions between different 'systems' within and beyond the individual (personal, familial, peer group, environmental, social and so on) and of developing interventions that target and work through these diverse systems to promote positive development. Thus, the Department of Health's (DH, 2000) well-known assessment framework for children in need and their families encourages social workers to look not only at the needs (and deeds) of the child or the young person, but at their interactions with their carers and with the wider world (see Figure 5.1).

Figure 5.1: The child's whole world

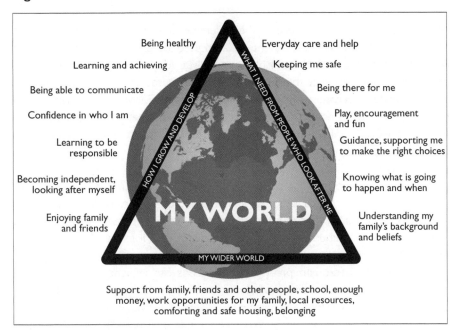

Source: DH, 2000

Here, admittedly in a policy field preoccupied with those deemed vulnerable rather than those deemed dangerous, the emphasis is on 'getting it right for every child' (Scottish Executive, 2004) – on children and young people's well-being and on their *well-becoming* (Aldgate, 2007).

As we have seen above, these self-same ideas are already at play in youth justice most notably in connection the growing popularity of MST, although perhaps they are also evident in the insistence of the practitioners in the Scottish survey to retain a holistic approach that prioritises welfare. Although it may be stretching the evidence, this may be a consequence of working in the context of a system (the Children's Hearings system) that was designed around a recognition that 'the vulnerable' and 'the dangerous' are overlapping groups not easily distinguished in practice (McDiarmid, 2005).

But what is more interesting still, I would suggest, is the (re-)emergence of developmental and ecological themes in approaches to offender rehabilitation (and risk management) in the adult field. Although the growing literature about desistance research and its implications for practice is relevant here (see Maruna, 2001; Farrall, 2002; McNeill, 2006), in this context the more obvious analogue is the 'Good Lives Model' (GLM) of offender rehabilitation, as developed by Tony Ward and his colleagues (Ward and Brown, 2004; Ward and Marshall, 2004; Ward and Gannon, 2006; Ward et al, 2007). Before going on to outline the main features of the GLM, it makes sense to first outline the limitations in the Risk-Needs-Responsivity (RNR) model of offender rehabilitation that the GLM aims to address. In this respect, Ward and Maruna (2007) provide an excellent summary of the main arguments.

Although it is difficult to do justice to RNR in further summarising Ward and Maruna's (2007) account of what is a set of interrelated theories about crime, offending and rehabilitation, their description of RNR is basically as follows. First, the core purpose of rehabilitation is to reduce the harms to the public caused by crime. Considerations of the offender's welfare are legitimate but secondary. Second, individuals vary in their propensity to commit crimes, so treatment should target those factors that are associated with offending. Third, the most important treatment targets are those that have been empirically demonstrated to reduce recidivism.

In terms of its aetiological implications, RNR proponents argue that an empirically informed theory of crime causation should be based on known risk factors, on their relationships with each other and on their relationship with actual incidents of crime. The 'proximal' (or immediate) cause of offending is the framing of an immediate situation by the offender in such a way that the rewards of offending outweigh the costs. Delinquent peers and pro-criminal attitudes can influence the offender in the situation to make offending more likely. More distal (or less immediate) causes of offending might include developmental adversity, growing up in an antisocial environment and lack of opportunity. Once an individual offends, the influence of these kinds of factors and problems is likely to be compounded. However, while background environmental factors (political, economic and cultural) can predispose someone towards offending, the more proximal factors discussed above must also be present for offending to occur.

The practice implications of RNR are well known. The principles are that:

- the level of service should be proportionate to the level of assessed risk (high-risk individuals require the most intensive intervention);
- the treatment should be focused on changing criminogenic needs (these being dynamic factors that, when changed, are associated with reduced recidivism);
- the style and mode of the intervention should engage the offender and suit their learning style and cognitive abilities.

These three principles require the development of comprehensive and validated assessment instruments to guide interventions and the development of treatment programmes that are cognitive behavioural in orientation, highly structured, implemented by well-trained, supported and supervised staff, delivered with integrity (in the manner intended by programme designers), based on manuals and located in organisations committed to rehabilitation in general and programmes in particular.

Ward and Maruna (2007) proceed to produce a detailed and balanced evaluation of RNR; only the six key messages are summarised here. First, RNR is vague about values and core principles (beyond a commitment to empiricism); hence its moral basis is under-developed. Second, and perhaps as a result, it fails to take account of the subjective and value-laden nature of concepts like 'risk' and 'harm', recasting 'needs' as 'dynamic risk factors'; it conceptualises risk in a highly individualised way, leading to offenders being construed essentially as the bearers of risk, irrespective of the social contexts that profoundly affect whether or not and in what ways 'riskiness' is ever realised. Third, a more practical problem with RNR's focus on risk and harm is that by focusing on the public interest, it neglects critical questions around offender motivation. Fourth, the narrow focus on risk and criminogenic need also leads to a neglect of the individual as a whole and their self-identity, despite the fact that personality psychologists now stress the importance of 'personal strivings' and 'self-narratives' as well as the 'traits' on which RNR focuses. Fifth, although RNR focuses on establishing the covariates of offending (and of reduced offending) in general to identify treatment targets, it does not really explain the relationships between risk and need factors and offending. Finally, Ward and Maruna (2007) stress that RNR has significant strengths and weaknesses as a practice theory; empirical support for the risk principle has been moderate but there is stronger support for the criminogenic need principle. With respect to responsivity, Ward and Maruna (2007) argue that while the notion of *general responsivity* (concerning which forms of treatment tend to suit offenders best) has received considerable attention (producing much support in general for the use of cognitive behavioural methods), questions of *individual responsivity* (concerning individual characteristics that affect successful engagement with intervention) require much further examination.

Overall, Ward and Maruna (2007) conclude that there is evidence that offenders treated according to RNR principles are more likely to desist, but they also report the findings of numerous 'what works' implementation studies (or programmes based on RNR) that point to problems and failings (see McNeill and Whyte 2007, chapter 8). Here, it is sufficient to note that Ward and Maruna (2007) suggest that it may be not that RNR is at fault in targeting risk, need and responsivity, but rather that the targeting of risk may be a *necessary* but not a *sufficient* condition for reducing reoffending. They suggest that to accommodate differences among offenders, a specific case formulation is required, rather than too generalised an application of the principles. Part of the task of formulation is not just to identify risk and needs, but to work out, case by case, how risks and needs interact to influence offending in specific contexts and, from such an understanding, how risks and needs can be best addressed. Finally, Ward and Maruna (2007) argue that RNR fails to attend adequately to key 'treatment' tasks concerning developing a 'therapeutic alliance' between the offender and the practitioner, and, more generally to issues of motivation. They point to evidence that offenders are more motivated by focusing on *approach goals* (promoting goods or personally endorsed adaptive goals) rather than *avoidance goals* (essentially not doing something) (Mann et al, 2004). Thus, focusing only on risk and criminogenic need may be counterproductive unless other methods to achieve goals are developed. Furthermore, although it may be correct that targeting criminogenic need is more effective in reducing reoffending, it might nonetheless be the case that targeting non-criminogenic need is sometimes a necessary precursor of doing so; offenders need to be receptive and attentive to interventions and may not be so if basic needs are not being effectively addressed.

In comparison to RNR, the GLM represents a relatively recent development in the field of offender rehabilitation (Ward and Brown, 2004; Ward and Marshall, 2004; Ward and Gannon, 2006; Ward et al, 2007). It draws on the developing field of 'positive psychology' to offer a strengths-based approach to rehabilitation: 'From the perspective of positive psychology, in order for individuals to desist from offending they should be given the knowledge, skills, opportunities and resources to live a 'good life', which takes into account their particular preferences, interests and values' (Ward and Maruna, 2007, p 111).

In setting out the general principles of the GLM, Ward and Maruna (2007) articulate several basic assumptions. Essentially, the GLM assumes that people (including offenders) are predisposed to seek certain goals or primary human goods. These goods have their sources in human nature and have evolved through natural selection to help people establish strong social networks and to survive and reproduce. They are prudential rather than moral goods and include, for example, life, knowledge, excellence in play and work, agency or autonomy, inner peace, friendship, community, spirituality, happiness and creativity. Secondary goods, such as certain types of work or relationships, provide particular ways and means for us to pursue and achieve primary goods. Because primary human goods are plural, there are many possible sources of motivation for human behaviour.

The GLM also rests on the assumption that interventions should aim to promote an individual's goods as well as to manage or reduce risk. A major aim of rehabilitative work is to enable an individual to develop a life plan that involves ways of effectively securing primary human goods without harming others. However, this is not just about tackling risk factors; it is about the holistic reconstruction of the self. Moreover, because human beings are complex and interdependent beings that function in a set of interrelated biological, psychological, social and environmental systems, practitioners need to consider and address individual, relational and contextual factors; attending to both characteristics and environments. Similarly, risk must be understood not as an attribute of offenders but in a multifaceted and contextualised way. Finally, the approach requires an explicit focus on conceptualising a good life; taking account of strengths, primary goods and relevant environments, and encouraging and respecting an individual's capacities to make choices for themselves – both as a moral principle (against enforced rehabilitation) and as a pragmatic one (that enforced rehabilitation cannot succeed).

In understanding the aetiology of offending, the GLM draws on strain theory to suggest that there are two basic routes to offending – direct and indirect. The direct route refers to situations where the individual seeks certain types of good through criminal activity. The indirect route refers to situations where the pursuit of a certain good has consequences that increase the pressure to offend; for example where the use of alcohol to relieve emotional pressure leads to a loss of control in particular circumstances. In the GLM, criminogenic needs are best understood as internal or external obstacles to the acquisition of primary human goods. In general, the aetiological assumptions of the GLM flow from:

> a naturalistic view of human beings as goal-seeking, culturally embedded animals who use a range of strategies to secure important goods from their environment. When the internal or external conditions necessary to achieve valued outcomes are incomplete, individuals tend to become frustrated and may engage in antisocial behaviour. (Ward and Maruna, 2007, p 124)

In the practice model that develops from these principles and assumptions, the practitioner must balance the promotion of personal goods (for the offender) with the reduction of risk (for society). Too strong a focus on personal goods may produce a happy but dangerous offender; but equally, too strong a focus on risk may produce a dangerously defiant or disengaged offender. The practitioner also has to create a human relationship in which the individual offender is valued and respected and through which interventions can be properly tailored in line with particular life plans and their associated risk factors. So, although, as with RNR, interventions should be structured and systematic, they should also be shaped to suit the person in question. The language used by the practitioner and their agency should be 'future-oriented, optimistic and approach goal focused' (Ward and Maruna, 2007, p 127) in order to foster motivation. Other considerations that underlie the construction of an action plan include the following:

- Prisoners and probationers as whole individuals are more than the sum of their criminal records; they have expertise and strengths that can benefit society and should be promoted.
- Many will have had adverse developmental experiences and will have lacked the opportunities and support necessary to develop a coherent life plan.
- Consequently, they may lack skills and capabilities that they need to achieve a fulfilling life.
- Criminal actions often represent attempts to achieve desired goods but where the skills or capabilities necessary to achieve them are missing (the direct route) or can arise from attempts to relieve the sense of incompetence and frustration that comes from not achieving valued human goods (the indirect route).
- The absence of certain human goods seems to be strongly associated with offending (for example, self-efficacy, agency, dignity, esteem, generativity).
- Risk may be reduced by developing the necessary skills and capabilities.
- Intervention should *enhance* an individual's repertoire rather than simply *removing or managing* a problem (see Ward and Maruna, 2007, pp 127-8).

In the process of assessment, Ward and Maruna (2007) suggest that as well as addressing risk, needs and responsivity, practitioners should also assess the individual's *priorities* – their goals, their life priorities and their aims for the intervention. This requires analysing the kinds of priorities implicit in their patterns of offending and also asking the person directly about what they value and where they place their efforts and energies. A more comprehensive assessment of an individual's potential for achieving a good life involves exploring:

- whether there is restricted scope for meeting some primary goods perhaps because of an undue focus on others;
- whether some goods are being pursued through inappropriate means;
- whether there is conflict between the individual's goals;
- whether the individual has the capacity or capabilities to enact their life plan and achieve their goals.

Case formulation proceeds by exploring presenting problems and criminogenic needs and then by establishing the function of the offending – that is, the primary human goods to which it directly or indirectly relates. It is also necessary to explore the 'overarching good' around which other goods or goals are oriented. Once the reasons for offending, the level of risk and the flaws in the individual's life plan have been understood, the practitioner should identify their strengths, positive experiences and expertise. Next, the effort shifts to exploring primary and secondary goods and how they might be better met. There should then follow some consideration of the individual's environment and its likely impact on their life plan, before in the final phase of assessment the practitioner constructs an intervention plan based on all of the above considerations:

> Thus, taking into account the kind of life that would be fulfilling and meaningful to the individual ... [the practitioner] notes the kinds of capabilities or competencies he or she requires to have a chance of putting that plan into action. A treatment plan is then developed. (Ward and Maruna, 2007, p 136)

Ward and Maruna's (2007) evaluation of the GLM presents a wealth of empirical evidence to support the theoretical frameworks, aetiological assumptions and practice foci of the model and points to positive evaluations of a number of correctional treatment programmes based on or analogous to the GLM. However, their candid conclusion is that:

> [t]he GLM appears to function well as an integrative framework, but so far there is a paucity of specific correctional programs that have been explicitly developed with GLM in mind. Thus there is a lack of direct, compelling research evidence for GLM-inspired programs. However, this is changing rapidly and, as we write, several correctional GLM programmes are being constructed and empirically evaluated. (Ward and Maruna, 2007, p 171)

Discussion

The GLM is at present an emergent model, and one which, like any theory, has its limitations. We might question, for example, whether the primary human goods are as universally pursued as the model suggests. Moreover, although the model recognises plurality among them, and the likelihood that different goods will be differently valued and prioritised by different individuals in different social contexts, it (at least as explained by Ward and Maruna, 2007) has relatively little to say about how practitioners should manage the deep tensions that exist in contemporary societies around diverse views of what constitutes the good life, and about the conflicts that arise in the pursuit of very different versions of that life within communities. In the contexts of both criminal and youth justice supervision, these tensions express themselves ultimately in problems of non-compliance. Although the stress on individualisation, engagement and motivation might be expected to foster compliance with supervision by both young people and adults, the question remains as to how non-compliance should be managed (see Robinson and McNeill, 2008).

At the individual level, we might also question whether all of those offenders with whom the probation service, youth justice and social workers engage would seek or require the holistic reconstruction of the self that the thoroughgoing revision of a good lives plan seems to suggest. Indeed, in thinking about applying the GLM specifically to young people, careful consideration needs to be given to their different developmental stages; their identities, aspirations and life plans are still developing and may be both less established and more mutable than those of adults.[5] Rather than requiring 'reconstruction', therefore, the challenge might be more appropriately focused on enabling young people to revise and reframe identities, aspirations and plans that are emergent rather than established. Although for those involved in serious or persistent offending and whose offending is clearly linked to and embedded in their emerging personal and social identities, intensive interventions may be required, as RNR recognises, less intensive or 'lighter touch' interventions might suffice in many cases. That said, there is no reason why the GLM would not allow for varying degrees of reconstruction and revision and indeed its emphasis on tailored intervention might require this.

A further problem is that, although the GLM recognises the importance of context as much as characteristics, it perhaps underplays the extent to which criminogenic social contexts (and limited life opportunities) might make a 'criminal' good lives plan logical and functional from the young person's point of view. A sharper focus on the importance of interventions around the familial and social contexts of offending and desistance, and on work to develop legitimate opportunities (or licit social capital; see Barry, 2006; McNeill and Whyte, 2007), might well be indicated.

It may be that the emphasis in both the RNR model and, to a lesser extent, the GLM model on within-individual analyses of, and responses to, offending is a consequence of the psychological orientation towards criminology in general and offender rehabilitation in particular that they share. That said, from a Scottish perspective, the GLM's values and principles seem highly consistent with social work's humanistic traditions, with its contemporary reliance on ecological perspectives, with its stress on the personalisation of care and with strengths-based perspectives.

Returning to debates about MAPPA and about children and young people involved in serious offending, it is ironic perhaps that I have looked to a model of *adult* offender rehabilitation in an effort to reassert the importance of social, developmental and ecological perspectives in thinking about – and beyond – risk assessment and risk management in youth justice. But perhaps this kind of conceptual excursion lends weight to the argument; if there is a growing recognition that reducing risk among serious adult offenders requires systems and practices that take account of and engage these perspectives, then the case in connection with children and young people is surely stronger still.

The salience and importance of these arguments and perspectives becomes clearer if we ask whether the dominance of the risk discourse might not be likely to frustrate its own purposes if it identifies young people with the worst aspects of themselves, if it leads practitioners to neglect their needs, strengths and goals, if it hinders genuine engagement between young people and practitioners and if it reinforces a social climate that creates practical and attitudinal barriers to young people's chances of leading good lives. One of the paradoxes of the risk society is that, in fact, we might all *be safer* and *feel safer* in a world where young people involved in serious offending were enabled and supported to develop good lives than in one where the risks that they present are merely managed and surveilled, and where those risks are continually reinforced by their stigmatisation and exclusion as risk bearers.

Notes

[1] I am grateful to Hugh McGregor of South Lanarkshire Council for permission to use material here from his recent presentation to the Glasgow Branch of the Scottish Association for the Study of Offending.

[2] The latest Scottish Government MAPPA guidance suggests that the arrangements will be extended to cover violent offenders by the end of 2009. See www.scotland. gov.uk/Publications

[3] The Risk Management Authority, which has no direct equivalent elsewhere in the UK, is a non-departmental public body that was established by the (then) Scottish Executive under Section 3 of the 2003 Criminal Justice (Scotland) Act to provide policy advice, identify best practice, set standards for risk assessment and management, accredit risk assessors and methods, approve offender risk management plans (in the most serious cases) and commission and undertake research.

[4] Children's Hearings are welfare tribunals headed by lay people from the local community. Children can be brought before a Hearing because they are beyond the control of their parents, are being exposed to moral danger, are likely to suffer unnecessarily or suffer serious impairment to health or development through lack of parental care, are the victim of a sex or cruelty offence, are failing to attend school regularly, are misusing drugs, alcohol or solvents, or have committed an offence. If the Hearing thinks that compulsory measures of supervision are appropriate in the best interests of the child, it will impose a supervision requirement, which may be renewed until the child becomes 18. For more details, see McDiarmid (2005).

[5] Since GLM is an emergent model, it is unsurprising that its development as a potential approach for use with younger offenders is at an early stage. Thus far, the focus has been on the salience of the GLM model for work with young people with sexually harmful behaviours (see Thakker et al, 2005; Collie et al, 2007). Practice projects in the UK and in New Zealand are currently developing work using GLM concepts and approaches.

References

Aldgate, J. (2007) 'Getting it right for every child: messages from research', a seminar presented at the Glasgow School of Social Work, 8 November, available from www.iriss.ac.uk/node/492

Barry, M. (2006) *Youth Offending in Transition: The Search for Social Recognition*, London: Routledge.

Bauman, Z. (2000) 'Social issues of law and order', *British Journal of Criminology*, vol 40, no 2, pp 205-21.

Boeck, T., Fleming, J. and Kemshall, H. (2006) 'The context of risk decisions: does social capital make a difference?', *Forum: Qualitative Social Research*, vol 7, no 1, article 17, available from www.qualitative-research.net/fqs-texte/1-06/06-1-17-e.htm

Burman, M., Armstrong, S., Batchelor, S., McNeill, F. and Nicholson, J. (2008) *Research and Practice in Risk Assessment and Risk Management of Children and Young People Engaging in Offending Behaviours*, Paisley: Risk Management Authority, available from www.rmascotland.gov.uk/

Burnett, R. and Roberts, C. (eds) (2004) *What Works in Probation and Youth Justice: Developing Evidence Based Practice*, Cullompton: Willan.

Cohen, S. (1985) *Visions of Social Control: Crime, Punishment and Classification*, Cambridge: Polity Press/Blackwell.

Collie, R., Ward, T., Hufham, L. and West, B. (2007) 'The Good Lives Model and young people who sexually offend', in M. Calder (ed) *Children and Young People who Sexually Abuse: Taking the Field Forward*, London: Russell House Publishing.

DH (Department of Health) (2000) *Framework for the Assessment of Children in Need and their Families*, London: DH, available from www.dh.gov.uk/en/Publicationsandstatistics/Publications/PublicationsPolicyAndGuidance/DH_4008144

Ericson, R. and Doyle, A. (eds) (2003) *Risk and Morality*, Toronto, Canada: University of Toronto Press.

Farrall, S. (2002) *Rethinking What Works with Offenders: Probation, Social Context and Desistance from Crime*, Cullompton: Willan.

Garland, D. (2001) *The Culture of Control: Crime and Social Order in Contemporary Society*, Oxford: Oxford University Press.

Gray, N., Laing, J. and Noaks, L. (2002) *Criminal Justice, Mental Health and the Politics of Risk*, London: Cavendish Publishing.

Hannah-Moffat, K. (2005) 'Criminogenic needs and the transformative risk subject: hybridizations of risk/need penality', *Punishment and Society*, vol 7, no 1, pp 29-51.

Hannah-Moffat, K. and Shaw, M. (2001) *Taking Risks: Incorporating Gender and Culture into Classification and Assessment of Federally Sentenced Women*, Ottawa, Canada: Status of Women Canada.

Hudson, B. (2001) 'Punishments, rights and difference: defending justice in the risk society', in K. Stenson and R. Sullivan (eds) *Crime, Risk and Justice: The Politics of Crime Control in Liberal Democracies* (pp 144-72), Cullompton: Willan.

Hudson, B. (2003) *Justice in the Risk Society*, London: Sage Publications.

Kemshall, H. (1998) 'Defensible decisions for risk: or "It's the doers wot get the blame"', *Probation Journal*, vol 45, no 2, pp 67-72.

Kemshall, H. (2003) *Understanding Risk in Criminal Justice*, Buckingham: Open University Press.

Laub, J. and Sampson, R. (2003) *Shared Beginnings, Divergent Lives: Delinquent boys to age 70*, Cambridge, MA: Harvard University Press.

McCulloch, P. and McNeill, F. (2007) 'Consumer society, commodification and offender management', *Criminology and Criminal Justice*, vol 7, no 3, pp 223-42.

McDiarmid, C. (2005) 'Welfare, offending and the Scottish children's hearings system', *Journal of Social Welfare and Family Law*, vol 27, no 1, pp 31-42.

McNeill, F. (2006) 'A desistance paradigm for offender management', *Criminology and Criminal Justice*, vol 6, no 1, pp 39-62.

McNeill, F. and Whyte, B. (2007) *Reducing Reoffending: Social Work and Community Justice in Scotland*, Cullompton: Willan.

Mann, R., Webster, S., Schofield, C. and Marshall, W. (2004) 'Approach versus avoidance goals in relapse prevention with sexual offenders', *Sexual Abuse: A Journal of Research and Treatment*, vol 16, no 1, pp 65-76.

Maruna, S. (2001) *Making Good: How Ex-Convicts Reform and Rebuild Their Lives*, Washington, DC: American Psychological Association.

O'Malley, P. (1999) *The Risk Society: Implications for Justice and Beyond*, Report Commissioned for the Department of Justice, Victoria, Australia: La Trobe University.

Robinson, G. (1999) 'Risk management and rehabilitation in the probation service: collision and collusion', *The Howard Journal of Criminal Justice*, vol 38, no 4, pp 421-33.

Robinson, G. (2002) 'Exploring risk management in probation practice: contemporary developments in England and Wales', *Punishment and Society*, vol 4, no 1, pp 5-26.

Robinson, G. and McNeill, F. (2008) 'The dynamics of compliance with community penalties', *Theoretical Criminology*, vol 12, no 4, pp 431-49.

Rose, N. (1998) 'Governing risky individuals: the role of psychiatry in new regimes of control', *Psychiatry, Psychology and the Law*, vol 5, no 2, pp 177-95.

Scottish Executive (2004) *Getting it Right for Every Child*, Edinburgh: Scottish Executive.

Silver, E. and Miller, L. (2002) 'A cautionary note on the use of actuarial risk assessment tools for social control', *Crime and Delinquency*, vol 48, no 1, pp 138-61.

Stenson, K. and Sullivan, R. (2001) *Crime, Risk and Justice: The Politics of Crime Control in Liberal Democracies*, Cullompton: Willan.

Thakker, J., Ward, T. and Tidmarsh, P. (2005) 'Relapse prevention with juvenile sex offenders: managing risk through the construction of better lives', in W. Marshall and H. Barbaree (eds) *The Juvenile Sex Offender* (2nd edition), New York: Guilford Press.

Ward, T. and Brown, M. (2004) 'The Good Lives Model and conceptual issues in offender rehabilitation', *Psychology, Crime & Law*, vol 10, no 3, pp 243-57.

Ward, T. and Gannon, T. (2006) 'Rehabilitation, etiology and self-regulation: the Good Lives Model of sexual offender treatment', *Aggression and Violent Behavior*, vol 11, no 1, pp 77-94.

Ward, T. and Marshall, W. (2004) 'Good Lives, aetiology and the rehabilitation of sex offenders: a bridging theory', *Journal of Sexual Aggression: Special Issue – Treatment and Treatability*, vol 10, no 2, pp 153-69.

Ward, T. and Maruna, S. (2007) *Rehabilitation: Beyond the Risk Paradigm*, London: Routledge.

Ward, T., Gannon, T. and Mann, R. (2007) 'The Good Lives Model of offender rehabilitation: clinical implications', *Aggression and Violent Behavior*, vol 12, no 1, pp 87-107.

MAPPA as 'risk in action': discretion and decision making

Kerry Baker

Introduction

At first sight, Multi-Agency Public Protection Arrangements (MAPPA) may appear to be an obvious example of the dominance of 'risk' in current criminal justice and penal policy. However, although risk-based governance (O'Malley, 2004) is clearly a significant feature of modern society, there are still 'unresolved struggles for pre-dominance between risk-based reasoning and other resources of knowledge, influence and prestige' (Loader and Sparks, 2007, p 85). This suggests that the implementation of risk-based ways of working can be affected by interaction with other practice paradigms, as well as factors such as organisational culture or the professional values of practitioners.

A related assumption that requires further consideration is the belief implicit in much of the guidance on MAPPA from the National Offender Management Service (NOMS) and the Youth Justice Board (YJB) that the introduction of a set of formalised procedures will lead to consistent and rigorous action that will reduce the risks to the public posed by some offenders (YJB, 2006; Ministry of Justice, 2007). Although the guidance is careful to avoid the claim that risk can be eliminated, there is an inherent expectation that procedural conformity will occur and will be beneficial. The reality is inevitably much more complex, however, with research showing considerable variation in practice both between different regions of the country and also between the adult and youth justice systems (Kemshall et al, 2005; Sutherland and Jones, 2008).

The impact of MAPPA is shaped both by its formal structures and by the day-to-day processes through which practitioners apply these requirements. This inevitably involves a combination of both rules (the prescribed framework) and discretion (such as decisions about individual cases that cannot be defined in guidance) or, in other words, a mixture of formal and informal practice. This is an area that has so far received little attention in the literature on MAPPA, yet it is an avenue that can help us understand issues such as the observed variance in practice or the impact of different professional cultures on the operation of MAPPA (Nash, 2006, 2007).

Just as understanding sentencing decisions requires an appreciation of the fact that they are 'socially produced and socially practised' (Tata, 2002, p 4), so a greater awareness of contextual factors is important for developing our understanding of MAPPA. This chapter therefore aims to explore topics such as the balance between rules and discretion in MAPPA, the significance of informal practice and some of the factors influencing decision making. Viewed in this way, MAPPA become a fascinating example of 'risk in action' in contemporary society. Furthermore, and perhaps of greater practical significance, this analysis also raises some important questions about the current MAPPA framework that should prompt further consideration of ways in which it could be developed so as to be more appropriate not only for young people but also for practitioners and managers in youth justice.

Rules and discretion: the MAPPA 'doughnut'

The importance of discretion in the operation of the criminal justice system is something that has long been recognised (see Hawkins, 1992) because 'however precise the law, theory or policy might be, there is always a certain flexibility, ambiguity or discretion in how it is applied in practice' (Gelsthorpe and Padfield, 2003, p 3).

Recently, there has been considerable debate as to whether the rise of managerialism and trends such as the increasing use of standardised risk assessment tools have limited professionals' scope for the exercise of professional judgement. In the social work field, Howe (1991) has written about the 'curtailment' of discretion while Ericson and Haggerty (1997, p 102), commenting more generally on the risk society, have argued that '[p]rofessionals are increasingly absent, their place taken by forms, computers, and step-by-step procedures that commodify expertise and reduce it to check-boxes, key-strokes, and self-help guides'. If 'autonomous decision making' is one of the key features of professional occupations (May and Buck, 1998, para 4.1), then some have seen these trends as an attack on practitioners' status and an attempt to turn them into mere rule-following technicians. Robinson (2003) has discussed the balance between technicality and indeterminacy in probation practice, while in youth justice there has been a corresponding and, at times polarised, debate as to whether or not practice has become deprofessionalised (Baker, 2005; Smith, 2007).

In starting to think about the role of professional discretion in relation to MAPPA, a number of questions spring to mind. How much discretion do the different participants (such as Youth Offending Team [YOT] workers, MAPPA coordinators, MAPPA chairs) currently have? How is this discretion exercised? Could it be used in inappropriate or discriminatory ways? Is there a case for increasing or decreasing the freedom for professional discretion? In order to answer such questions, it is necessary first to consider what is meant by the term 'discretion'.

The nature of professional discretion

A weakness in much of the debate about practice in youth justice has been the absence of discussion about the nature of discretion. First, it can too easily be assumed that professional discretion must be a positive feature of practice whereas, as Evans and Harris (2004) helpfully suggest, discretion in itself is neither good nor bad but rather is something that can be exercised in a variety of ways, some of which may be inappropriate (for example if it is used to reinforce biased or discriminatory practice). The value of discretion therefore depends on how it is used and applied.

Second, there are different types of discretion: 'judgement that has to be employed to apply a standard (in circumstances where judgement cannot be applied mechanically); the final responsibility for making a decision (within the rules); and discretion in a strong sense, which gives the decisions and the criteria of decision making to professionals' (Dworkin, cited in Evans and Harris, 2004, p 881). Thus, in situations where rules are prescribed such that professionals might not have 'strong' discretion, they can still have 'weaker' discretion, that is, 'interpretation of and authority to decide within rules' (Evans and Harris, 2004, p 882). To take an example from current youth justice practice in England and Wales, initiatives that might appear to be very prescriptive (such as National Standards) need not lead to the removal of all discretion in themselves but rather 'it is their *interpretation* which determines whether they become a managerialist or professional tool' (Eadie and Canton, 2002, p 16; emphasis added). Consequently, the debate about discretion should not be couched in 'all-or-nothing' terms but instead needs to recognise that different decision-making points will involve varying amounts and types of discretion.

Third, professional discretion and rules are not opposites. Rather, discretion and judgement are always exercised within a framework of requirements or, to put it more vividly, '[d]iscretion, like the hole in a doughnut, does not exist except as an area left open by a surrounding belt of restriction' (Dworkin, 1978, p 31). That is to say, no decisions – including those made in relation to MAPPA – are ever made with complete freedom but always within certain boundary limits.

A mixed economy

The operation of MAPPA in England and Wales is currently based on a combination of some very prescriptive 'rules' together with freedom for practitioners to exercise discretion at certain stages of the process (Ministry of Justice, 2007). For example, the prescriptiveness of MAPPA is seen in:

* the definition of categories 1 and 2 (inclusion in these groups is automatically triggered by offence and/or sentencing criteria);
* the requirement on YOTs to notify MAPPA of all cases in categories 1 and 2;

- the requirement for data about MAPPA cases to be entered onto the Violent and Sex Offender Register (ViSOR);
- the requirement to consider disclosure in every case.

On the other hand, there is scope for exercising professional discretion in:

- judgements about whether an offender meets the criteria for category 3;
- decisions by MAPPA coordinators on acceptance/rejection of referrals for risk management at level 2 or 3;
- decisions in MAPP meetings about the level of risk management required;
- decisions about whether or not to disclose information to third parties;
- decisions about the resources required for an appropriate risk management plan.

This list (which is by no means exhaustive) illustrates not only the mix of prescription and freedom within MAPPA but also different types of discretion as discussed above.[1] The various 'players' within MAPPA are involved at different stages of the decision-making process and it is therefore likely that, for example, a YOT worker's perception of the rules/discretion balance will be different to that of a MAPPA coordinator or chair.

The right balance?

In considering the suitability of the current MAPPA framework in England and Wales for young people, one useful perspective is therefore to look at the balance between rules and discretion or, using Dworkin's metaphor, the relative proportions of the substance and the hole in the MAPPA doughnut.

In some areas, the balance appears to be appropriate, for example in relation to questions about disclosure of information. 'Consideration must be given in each case as to whether disclosure of information about an offender to others should take place to protect victims, potential victims, staff and other persons in the community' (Ministry of Justice, 2007, p 33). The guidance lists a number of factors that should be considered (see also Kemshall and Wood, this volume), which include taking account of the impact of disclosure on the offender. The government appears to have resisted considerable pressure for disclosure to occur in every case (see Nash, 2006). Instead, the guidance prudently combines both prescription (such as the expectation that disclosure will be considered in all cases and the requirement that reasons for decisions should be recorded in MAPP meeting minutes) with freedom for the professionals involved to determine the most appropriate course of action in each case.

As an example of where the balance may be less appropriate, however, consider, second, the question of who is included in MAPPA. All young people meeting the criteria for categories 1 and 2 should be notified to MAPPA even though the majority of them will continue to be managed at level 1 in line with normal YOT case management procedures.

In contrast to this automaticity, the model currently being introduced in Northern Ireland – known as Public Protection Arrangements Northern Ireland (PPANI) – allows for much more discretion in the case of young people. The categories and levels are similar to those used in England and Wales but PPANI explicitly acknowledge the distinction between young people and adults. A young person who meets the eligibility criteria *can* be referred to PPANI but does not have to be. There is no automatic trigger but rather it is up to the professionals working with the young person to decide if this would be appropriate. If the case can be managed appropriately through normal supervision requirements then there is no expectation of PPANI involvement but if, in exceptional cases, there is a clear benefit to be gained from more active multi-agency involvement (such as additional resources) then staff dealing with the young person have the discretion to choose that route (Northern Ireland Office, 2008).

If the issue of referral to MAPPA is one where it would be possible to argue for more discretion, then questions about how young people are treated once they are 'in' MAPPA raise the opposite question of whether the reliance on 'informal' good practice allows too much discretion. There is little distinction between adults and young people in terms of the *formal* rules and procedures, for example the criteria for categories 1 and 2 are the same, as are the requirements in relation to recording of data on ViSOR. The most recent national guidance (Ministry of Justice, forthcoming) does, however, recommend that MAPPA coordinators and chairs deal with young people differently. For example, the guidance acknowledges some of the challenges of assessing risk in a young person whose behaviour may change rapidly during adolescence and also states that MAPPA have to take account of a young person's needs as well as of the risk they may present to others. The guidance also highlights that there are specific considerations to take into account when deciding on disclosure of information, such as a young person's statutory right to education.

But what does this mean in practice? How will it happen and how do we know that these additional factors are being considered appropriately? Under the current framework for England and Wales, the development of systems and procedures that take account of the particular needs of young people will be heavily reliant on the goodwill of local MAPPA coordinators and chairs. This is likely to lead to pockets of good practice in some areas but not necessarily a widespread improvement. This could also be a problem in Scotland where, although the legislation is framed specifically with adults in mind, there is potential for MAPPA to be *informally* extended to include young people (see McNeill, this volume). If this kind of unofficial application of MAPPA were to occur, perhaps without some of the formal rules being applied, there is clearly potential for both the procedures and the outcomes to be inappropriate for young people.

Thus, freedom and the ability to exercise professional judgement can have both benefits and disadvantages and determining the right balance of rules and discretion is rarely straightforward. However, this discussion prompts the question of whether it would be possible and/or desirable to have a framework that allows practitioners more discretion about which young people are referred to MAPPA, but that also perhaps provides more 'rules' about how young people are dealt with once they become part of the system so as to help ensure that their needs and rights are taken seriously.

Professionals and decision making

'Those involved in decision-making processes experience a considerable degree of mandated flexibility in the decisions they can make about individuals and this immediately draws attention to uncertainties and anxieties about discretion' (Gelsthorpe and Padfield, 2003, p 1). The question of how decisions are made – in effect, how the players in MAPPA are exercising discretion – is important because of the significant impact that MAPPA can have on individual offenders. It is also important to bear in mind the 'serial conception of criminal justice decision making' (Hawkins, 2003, p 196), that is to say, decisions at one stage of the process affect decisions made at subsequent stages.[2] This gives added significance to the importance of each decision as, for example, assessments made by the YOT when referring a case will affect judgements made further down the line by representatives of other agencies involved in MAPPA.

> The combination of discretion, rule application, and the principally undetermined character of what *the professional* will be confronted with, presupposes a degree of trust in his or her competence to produce desired responses, and to deal with situations that may be exceptional in a sensible and creative way. (Hupe and Hill, 2007, p 282; emphasis added)

In looking at how decisions are made within MAPPA, it is necessary to also consider the implications of MAPPA participants being 'professionals'. There is not space here to provide anything other than a very brief summary, but various writers have identified factors such as autonomy, distinct knowledge or expertise, and credentialism as key characteristics of professionals (Friedson, 1994; Eadie, 2000). How are these evident in MAPPA decision making?

Autonomy and street-level bureaucracy

Surprisingly perhaps, the concept of 'street-level bureaucracy' (Lipsky, 1980) appears to have had relatively little attention in discussions about decision making by criminal justice practitioners in England and Wales.[3] In analysing the way in which workers experience and interpret organisational rules, Lipsky highlights the conflicts caused for individuals working in situations of high need with insufficient resources and in organisational structures that may not be consistent with their values or ideals. In addition, street-level bureaucrats (in contrast to top-level administrators or policy makers) have to deal with the 'clients' personal reactions to their decisions' (1980, p 9).

This complexity of day-to-day practice means that frontline staff cannot just apply rules in a straightforward way but rather, Lipsky argues, practitioners inevitably have to resort to shortcuts, compromises and routines, with the result that policy 'is actually made in the crowded offices and daily encounters of street-level workers' (1980, p xii). For example, the way in which practitioners use their time, allocate resources or make decisions about providing or withholding information all affect the way in which a service is delivered and the end result may be different to that intended by senior managers or politicians. The use of autonomy and discretion thus 'relates to differences between what is said to be the case or what might be the case, and what *is* the case; the formal position and the actual practice' (Gelsthorpe and Padfield, 2003, p 3; emphasis in original).

The role of YOT practitioners in relation to MAPPA may at first sight appear to be clearly defined and seemingly straightforward. When dealing with a young person who meets the MAPPA eligibility criteria, the expected course of action would look something like the following (YJB, 2006; Sutherland and Jones, 2008):

- complete the core *Asset* profile and Risk of Serious Harm (ROSH) form;
- discuss with manager and/or internal YOT risk management panel;
- notify/refer to MAPPA using standardised forms;
- provide risk assessment(s) and other information to MAPPA as required.

As street-level bureaucrats, practitioners will be faced with a number of tensions, which could include some or all of the following:

- lack of time;
- high caseloads;
- unclear local policies or procedures;
- ideological objections to describing young people as presenting a high risk of serious harm to others;
- concerns over the reaction of potentially violent and volatile young people to being told that they are subject to MAPPA.

Although the prescribed procedures may seem straightforward to apply, there are numerous points in the process where practitioners can interpret the rules to suit their own preferred ways of working or to help them cope with practice tensions. For example, assessors can complete the 'indicators of serious harm' section of the core *Asset* profile in such a way so as not to trigger a full ROSH assessment. Or, in cases where young people clearly meet the criteria for MAPPA categories 1 or

2, YOTs may deliberately choose to keep cases at level 1 because of a reluctance to label young people as a risk to others. While some of the variability between YOTs in applying what on paper appear to be fairly clear criteria and procedures will be attributable to factors such as differences in local offender populations between areas (see Sutherland, this volume), street-level decisions by practitioners will also be highly significant.

Multi-tiered decision making

In understanding the impact of organisational structure and culture on decision making, it is also helpful to remember that street-level bureaucrats work within a network of both horizontal relationships (colleagues within their agency, peers in similar organisations, professional associations) and vertical ones (offenders, managers, political leaders). In the context of MAPPA, this 'multiple accountability' (Hupe and Hill, 2007, p 290) becomes more complex with additional requirements to work with and be answerable to professionals from a range of different organisations.

Decision making in MAPPA is both serial and multi-tiered. Discussion of street-level bureaucracy has typically focused on the roles of frontline workers and managers, but within MAPPA there are other roles to consider. MAPPA coordinators or members of screening panels are not directly involved in the case management of individual offenders, but are responsible for decisions regarding categorisation and thresholding of cases which will have an impact on subsequent decisions about resource provision and the stringency of risk management conditions. Senior managers attending MAPP meetings are another step removed from everyday case management but still face considerable dilemmas of having to make decisions about individual cases in a context of resource constraints, political pressure and high (possibly unrealistic) expectations from the media and the public.[4]

There would appear to be a need for further research concerning decision making at these different levels in the context of a multi-agency practice environment. For example, understanding how YOT practitioners, as street-level bureaucrats, experience the process of having decisions accepted or rejected by representatives from other agencies whom they may perceive as having little understanding of the needs of young people may be important as a first step in finding ways to improve the YOT/MAPPA interface.

Having and using expert knowledge

If it is the case that professionals have 'a number of key identifiable traits, one of which is autonomous decision making, underscored by a *distinct, theoretical, expert knowledge base*' (May and Buck, 1998, para 4.1; emphasis added), then the application of MAPPA to young people raises some important questions. To what extent is there a clear knowledge base about public protection? More specifically, how developed is the knowledge base around the assessment and management of young people who commit serious sexual and violent offences? And, critically, how do practitioners and other decision makers use the knowledge that they have?

Although the knowledge base about young people who commit serious offences is expanding (Borum and Verhaagen, 2006; Burman et al, 2008; Grimshaw et al, 2008), it is clear that there are still significant gaps in the literature, for example in relation to violence (see McNeill, this volume). Kemshall and Wood (this volume) identify some of the principles of risk management that can reasonably be transferred from the adult world to youth justice but elsewhere have also highlighted the limitations of existing knowledge (Kemshall, 2007).

There is, then, the question of how such knowledge as does exist is communicated to, and understood by, practitioners. Evidence from child protection inquiries suggests that social workers often 'have an inadequate grasp of the *theoretical knowledge* needed to make sense of the information they gather' (Munro, 1998, p 92; emphasis added). Research relating to YOT workers' assessments of risk of serious harm found that few if any practitioners explicitly referred to theory as being an influence on their decision making (Baker, 2008).

Studies in social work, probation and youth justice that have looked at how practitioners interpret information (Munro, 1998; Baker, 2008) have shown that, while some assessors generated a number of hypotheses about individual cases and compared these in order to find the best 'fit' with the available evidence, others remained fixed with 'one particular idea about how the situation was to be understood, or no particular idea at all' (Sheppard et al, 2001, p 871). In the context of probation practice, Kemshall (1998, p 159) found that the process of generating and falsifying hypotheses was the exception rather than the rule and instead 'the mode of inquiry appears to reflect ... the closed professional system in which information is matched to existing beliefs'. Baker (2007) also found that youth justice practitioners were concerned about locating a 'right answer' and were reluctant to speculate about possible future alternative behaviours.

If assessors were considering multiple hypotheses then, as Sheppard (1995, p 275) suggests, they would be alert to 'disconfirming data' and ready to reformulate hypotheses in the light of new evidence. But why is this so rarely seen in practice? Perhaps it is partly because of the perception of a blame culture in which practitioners fear that speculating about a variety of possible options could be seen as indicating a lack of competence in reaching decisions about risk levels. It might also be to do with the fact that an assessor cannot just reconsider one item of information

> but has to consider changing the whole picture of the case. All the known evidence then needs to be reappraised and found a place in the new emerging picture. The human tendency to avoid critical reappraisals of their beliefs may in part be due to

reluctance to undertake such *a challenging and arduous intellectual task.* (Munro, 1996, p 800; emphasis added)

This task can be made even more difficult if practitioners are required to use technology that does not allow for easy revision of information and which, more broadly, may prioritise data over knowledge (Aas, 2004).

In addition, there is an understandable temptation for practitioners working in complex situations to seek certainty, which may result in a reluctance to consider alternative hypotheses (Baker, 2008). However, it has been argued that, because of the difficulty involved in making assessments of risk, 'practitioners need to stay in uncertainty for longer, and to assess whether, because of the circumstances, there is a need to hold on to doubt whilst taking the time to seek out other possible versions' (Taylor and White, 2006, p 944). There is thus a very difficult dilemma between the need to remain open to new information while at the same time being required to make decisions in order to inform practical action.

The discussion so far has focused on the practice of individual workers in making decisions. Can MAPPA, which require organisations to share responsibility for assessment and management of risk to the public, help alleviate some of these difficulties? There are pluses and minuses. In terms of professional knowledge, it may be that the pooled expertise of representatives of different agencies helps to ensure that assessments are more theoretically grounded. Feedback from MAPPA to individual practitioners may be one way to help them 'use theory or research findings to shake up or destabilize precipitously formed judgments' (Taylor and White, 2006, p 946). On the other hand, if there are conflicting knowledges within single organisations (Kemshall, 2000) then there will inevitably be competing knowledges within MAPPA. If the predominant culture is adult based then it is possible that decisions taken by MAPPA could reflect inappropriate analysis of information if based on theoretical perspectives or research findings with untested applicability to young people.

By sharing responsibility, MAPPA may enable individual workers to be less defensive in their practice if they know that they will not be held solely accountable in the case of something going wrong. In addition, MAPPA can have an important role in challenging assessments made by individual workers and agencies (see Kemshall and Wood, this volume). On the other hand, MAPPA may in some cases reinforce weak decisions if there is a collective unwillingness to look at alternative hypotheses or to admit previous errors. Multi-agency working will not of itself necessarily lead to better decision making (Rumgay, 2007). It may do, but only if adequate attention is given to further development of the knowledge base and if there is a shared willingness to consider multiple hypotheses and to live with a degree of uncertainty.

Exclusionary or inclusive risk-based practice?

The recent focus on actuarial justice, with its emphasis on categorising groups of offenders and its association with incapacitative prison warehousing and legislation such as 'three strikes', has perhaps contributed to the view that risk-based approaches are inevitably antithetical to constructive engagement with offenders. In this view,

> [b]y centring insecurity and threat, the governmental grid of risk is seen to work through negation: certain persons are defined primarily in terms of their purely negative and dangerous status as threats to others (victims), and accordingly are merely neutralised and segregated in new gulags of incapacitation. (O'Malley, 2004, p 143)

Does a focus on risk necessarily lead to deficit-based approaches to working with offenders, however, or is it possible to combine an emphasis on risk management with more rehabilitative and inclusive practice? Professional discretion and decision making are again critical here in determining the consequences for offenders of their involvement in MAPPA. Neither national nor local guidance can specify the actions that should be taken to manage risk in individual cases and this leaves freedom for MAPPA participants to adopt a variety of exclusionary or inclusive approaches. There are limited data available on the types of interventions or services specified in MAPPA risk management plans for young people, hence this section being less detailed and more tentative than the preceding discussions, but it is nevertheless useful to try to tease out some of the ways in which professional discretion affects offenders' experiences of MAPPA.

The contested terrain of 'risk'

So far in this chapter, the term 'risk' has been used in a way that implicitly reflects the idea that it is something calculable and perhaps controllable. This type of 'probabilistic discourse' (Kemshall, 2002, p 15), although dominant in government and policy thinking, is not the only concept of risk currently in circulation (Brown, 2000). For example, Loader and Sparks (2007, p 94; emphasis in original) suggest that 'when we speak of *risk* we are not generally alluding to the calculation of probabilities *stricto sensu*. We are talking also about ways of *representing* risky topics, people, and places and this generally suggests an active and often impassioned disposition towards them'. This is resonant with the idea of a populist 'criminology of the other, of the threatening outcast' (Garland, 1996, p 461). Another perspective is that of Parton (2001) who has argued that instead of conceptualising risk in terms of calculative probability, it should be viewed much more in terms of uncertainty.

What is the significance of this for practice? A concept of risk based on fear of the 'other' might be more likely to lead to exclusionary practices whereas a calculative probability-based approach may be more amenable to the possibility of inclusive strategies (or potentially at least for those assessed as 'lower risk'). The language and policy of MAPPA is predominantly that of a rational calculative approach but that does not mean that all participants will share a common concept of risk. Neither can practitioners and managers be totally immune from the social swirl of moral panic that demonises certain groups or behaviours. Consequently, pressure for exclusionary or inclusive practices may vary over time or between different MAPPA areas depending on individual perceptions and reactions to current events. In addition, while risk is clearly a significant influence on criminal justice policy and practice, it is not the only game in town (Kemshall, 2002; Loader and Sparks, 2007). Risk competes for position alongside other paradigms such as restorative justice, human rights and welfare so that the working out of risk-based practices varies in ways that reflect different social and political cultures (O'Malley, 2004).

In such a context, '[t]he distinction that now becomes more critical is not that between welfare versus risk. Rather, it is between those risk-based strategies that are inclusive in their aims and effects (which would include most of the risk–welfare hybrids), and those that are exclusionary and seek to reduce risk by merely isolating and incapacitating those identified as risk creators' (O'Malley, 2004, p 136). MAPPA could be categorised as a hybrid risk model as illustrated, for example, by the way in which the importance of disclosure of information for risk management purposes is balanced with a recognition of the need to avoid stigmatisation or retribution against the offender. A purely exclusionary approach is therefore less likely to occur if there is an acceptance of the need to consider welfare and human rights as well as risk.

Day-to-day practice

If MAPPA can thus be construed as a risk–welfare hybrid then there is scope for inclusive and rehabilitative practice, but whether or not offenders experience this in terms of the day-to-day operation of MAPPA depends on how the professionals involved apply discretion in their decision making.

Participation by young people in the MAPPA process

Current national guidance makes clear that offenders should not attend MAPP meetings but emphasises that they should be included in the process in other ways:

> Offenders (and, in the case of young people, their parents) should not become abstracted from the process of assessing and managing the risks they present. It is good practice for offenders to know that they are being managed through MAPPA, what MAPPA is and what this means for them. (Ministry of Justice, 2007, p 19)

Wood and Kemshall (2007, p 16) found, in respect of adults, that the provision of accessible information about MAPPA 'supported by individualised "contracts" of supervision' helped offenders to understand the role of MAPPA and their obligations to comply. Current practice in youth justice appears to be rather mixed. Although some YOTs try to clearly explain MAPPA to young people, there are examples of teams who have deliberately chosen not to do this on the grounds that it 'might be counterproductive to what [MAPPA are] trying to achieve' (Sutherland and Jones, 2008, p 32). Such an approach will need to be challenged given the clear expectations from NOMS and the YJB about the importance of engagement.

As well as understanding the purpose of MAPPA, offenders should also be given an opportunity to present information to MAPP meetings, either in writing or through a case manager/supervising officer. Youth Offending Team practitioners may need to work intensively and creatively to enable young people to contribute meaningfully to the MAPPA process and to express their views clearly. This will be a critical factor affecting the extent to which young people are able to participate and is very much dependent on the skills, attitudes and ability to engage of individual practitioners. To date, there has been no research that has asked young people about their perceptions of MAPPA, their experiences of it or the extent to which they feel able to participate and this must surely be an important issue for future consideration.

Exhortations from NOMS to the effect that '[o]ffenders should not only be seen as part of the problem as they can be a very important part of the solution in protecting the public' (Ministry of Justice, 2007, p 20) will only have a meaningful practical impact if practitioners use professional discretion in ways that enable young people to take some 'ownership' of the change process. An interesting question here would be whether insights from strengths-based approaches (see McNeill, this volume) can be incorporated into work with young people under MAPPA supervision (that is, be an example of a risk–welfare hybrid) or whether they can only be used as alternatives to risk-focused models.

Interventions

In addition to the broader picture of informing young people about MAPPA and helping them to participate where possible, there is also the question of the exclusionary or inclusive nature of particular interventions. As Kemshall and Wood (2007, p 391) have noted, 'risk management can be divided into two basic approaches: the coercive and integrative'. In the context of MAPPA, coercive could refer to strategies such as surveillance whereas an example of integrative measures (at least with adults) would be 'circles of support'.[5]

Putting together a risk management plan is one of the key areas of discretion for MAPPPs and decisions about what to include in a plan will be influenced by a range of factors including organisational cultures, resource availability, risk aversion and the success or failure of previous cases. Given both the potential of risk–welfare hybrid models to permit a focus on inclusion and the requirement on MAPPA agencies to consider the welfare of young people, there is surely an argument for saying that risk management plans should include elements that facilitate rehabilitation (this may be in addition to, not instead of, other measures for control, such as surveillance or tagging).

There is currently no information available on the content of MAPPA risk management plans for young people, which makes it difficult to comment on the exclusionary or inclusive nature of interventions with this group. Anecdotally, however, youth justice practitioners have reported examples of MAPP meetings rejecting plans with a reintegrative or restorative justice focus (even though the YOT may have secured agreement from the relevant agencies), but more evidence in this area is required.

It will be interesting to see how practice develops in Northern Ireland as MAPPA are implemented. The youth justice system there has a much more explicit focus on inclusion, participation and restorative justice than is apparent in England and Wales (Youth Justice Agency, 2007). Will the imposition of a risk-based approach such as MAPPA into this existing practice context result in more punitive and exclusionary interventions for young people or will practitioners retain existing values and continue to work in inclusive ways?

Conclusion

MAPPA are a fascinating example of 'risk in action'. They combine elements of the new penology, such as classifying offenders into management groups by risk level, with a more traditional (or perhaps clinical) focus on individualised assessment and tailored interventions. The practical difficulties in YOT–MAPPA interaction and some of the philosophical and ethical questions about the application of the MAPPA framework for young people have all been explored by contributors to this volume. In trying both to help explain some of these difficulties and to identify some avenues for future policy and practice development, this chapter has focused on rules, discretion and decision making and the ways in which they influence how MAPPA operate.

'Discretion is always embedded in a rule structure' (Hupe and Hill, 2007, p 281) and various examples of the balance between rules and discretion in MAPPA decision making have been discussed. In concluding, one obvious question is therefore whether the current MAPPA 'doughnut' in relation to young people in England and Wales is rightly proportioned. For example, why do level 1 cases all have to be notified to MAPPA (and at some future date, entered onto ViSOR) if the majority of them are assessed as relatively low risk and able to be appropriately supervised through normal YOT procedures? Is there not an argument for considering the Northern Ireland approach of enabling young people to be referred to MAPPA where there are clear benefits of doing so while allowing staff the freedom not to refer cases if they can be managed in other ways? If politicians and/or policy makers are not willing to allow practitioners to make such decisions, it would seem to imply not only a continued fear of young people but also a lack of trust in the professionalism of youth justice workers.

Some might argue that, in view of the evidence from child protection, probation and youth justice on practitioners' decision making, policy makers are right to be cautious about allowing the use of professional discretion in this area. Whatever the precise shape of the risk management doughnut, however, there will always and inevitably need to be scope for discretion given the vagaries and uncertainties of young people's behaviour. For YOT practitioners and MAPPA participants, the 'essential 'blur' at the centre of their enterprise' (Gelsthorpe and Padfield, 2003, p 15) will remain, that is to say, the need to make difficult judgements about the likelihood of individual young people causing serious harm to others. Now that the procedures of MAPPA have been refined and standardised (Ministry of Justice, 2007), more attention needs to be given to staff skills and knowledge (Nash, 2006) and to enabling decision makers to live with uncertainty.

Given that MAPPA are likely to be a significant feature of the public protection landscape for the foreseeable future (with some degree of variance across the UK), is it too much to hope that if more consideration was given as to how best to deal with young people who present a risk to others there might also be benefits for adult offenders? Despite the reluctance of some MAPPA participants to acknowledge the need for young people to be treated differently, the statutory requirements on agencies to have regard to the welfare of children and young people perhaps bring into clearer focus the importance of rehabilitation and reintegration. If there was a greater willingness to consider inclusive approaches for young people and if decision makers were more skilled and confident in using professional discretion to develop rigorous but creative risk management strategies, then there may in turn be wider benefits if MAPPA decision making could in future be characterised as risk attentive rather than risk averse.

Notes

[1] In addition, there will also have been a mix of prescription and discretion in decisions preceding those listed here; for example, the risk assessment undertaken by the YOT prior to a case being referred to MAPPA is prescribed in that practitioners have to use the *Asset* framework, but they have considerable discretion in collecting and analysing information to complete the assessment.

[2] This issue was highlighted by a review into the case of Anthony Rice, an offender who committed murder while under probation supervision and subject to MAPPA (HMIP, 2006).

[3] Street-level bureaucrats as described by Lipsky (1980, p xi) include teachers, the police, social workers, court officers and others who 'interact with and have wide discretion over the dispensation of benefits or the allocation of public sanctions'.

[4] The term 'first-floor bureaucrats' has been used to refer to groups such as middle-ranking policy makers (Page and Jenkins, 2005, p 7) but it could also be aptly applied to roles such as these.

[5] See www.circles-uk.org.uk/

References

Aas, K.F. (2004) 'From narrative to database: technological change and penal culture', *Punishment and Society*, vol 6, no 4, pp 379-93.

Baker, K. (2005) 'Assessment in youth justice: professional discretion and the use of Asset', *Youth Justice*, vol 5, no 2, pp 106-22.

Baker, K. (2008) 'Risk, uncertainty and public protection: assessment of young people who offend', *British Journal of Social Work*, vol 38, no 8, pp 1463-80.

Borum, R. and Verhaagen, D. (2006) *Assessing and Managing Violence Risk in Juveniles*, New York: The Guilford Press.

Brown, M. (2000) 'Calculations of risk in contemporary penal practice', in M. Brown and J. Pratt (eds) *Dangerous Offenders: Punishment and Social Order* (pp 93-108), London: Routledge.

Burman, M., Armstrong, S., Batchelor, S., McNeill, F. and Nicholson, J. (2008) *Research and Practice in Risk Assessment and Risk Management of Children and Young People Engaging in Offending Behaviours*, Paisley: Risk Management Authority.

Dworkin, R. (1978) *Taking Rights Seriously*, London: Duckworth.

Eadie, T. (2000) 'From befriending to punishing: changing boundaries in the probation service', in N. Malin (ed) *Professionalism, Boundaries and the Workplace* (pp 161-77), London: Routledge.

Eadie, T. and Canton, R. (2002) 'Practising in a context of ambivalence: the challenge for youth justice workers', *Youth Justice*, vol 2, no 1, pp 14-26.

Ericson, R. and Haggerty, K. (1997) *Policing the Risk Society*, Toronto, Canada: University of Toronto Press.

Evans, T. and Harris, J. (2004) 'Street-level bureaucracy, social work and the (exaggerated) death of discretion', *British Journal of Social Work*, vol 34, no 6, pp 871-95.

Friedson, E. (1994) *Professionalism Reborn: Theory, Prophecy and Policy*, Cambridge: Polity Press.

Garland, D. (1996) 'The limits of the sovereign state: strategies of crime control in contemporary society', *British Journal of Criminology*, vol 36, no 4, pp 445-71.

Gelsthorpe, L. and Padfield, N. (2003) 'Introduction', in L. Gelsthorpe and N. Padfield (eds) *Exercising Discretion: Decision-Making in the Criminal Justice System and Beyond* (pp 1-28), Cullompton: Willan.

Grimshaw, R. with Malek, M., Oldfield, M. and Smith, R. (2008) *Young People who Sexually Abuse (Source Document)*, London: YJB.

Hawkins, K. (1992) *The Uses of Discretion*, Oxford: Clarendon Press.

Hawkins, K. (2003) 'Order, rationality and silence: some reflections on criminal justice decision-making', in L. Gelsthorpe and N. Padfield (eds) *Exercising Discretion: Decision-Making in the Criminal Justice System and Beyond* (pp 186-219), Cullompton: Willan.

HMIP (Her Majesty's Inspectorate for Probation) (2006) *An Independent Review of a Serious Further Offence Case: Anthony Rice*, London: HMIP.

Howe, D. (1991) 'Knowledge, power and the shape of social work practice', in M. Davies (ed) *The Sociology of Social Work* (pp 202-20), London: Routledge.

Hupe, P. and Hill, M. (2007) 'Street-level bureaucracy and public accountability', *Public Administration*, vol 85, no 2, pp 279-99.

Kemshall, H. (1998) *Risk in Probation Practice*, Aldershot: Ashgate.

Kemshall, H. (2000) 'Conflicting knowledge on risk: the case of risk knowledge in the probation service', *Health, Risk and Society*, vol 2, no 2, pp 143-58.

Kemshall, H. (2002) *Risk, Social Policy and Welfare*, Buckingham: Open University Press.

Kemshall, H. (2007) 'Risk assessment and risk management: the right approach?', in M. Blyth, E. Solomon and K. Baker (eds) *Young People and 'Risk'* (pp 7-23), Bristol: The Policy Press.

Kemshall, H. and Wood, J. (2007) 'High risk offenders and public protection', in L. Gelsthorpe and R. Morgan (eds) *Handbook of Probation* (pp 381-97), Cullompton: Willan.

Kemshall, H., Mackenzie, G., Wood, J., Bailey, R. and Yates, J. (2005) *Strengthening Multi-Agency Public Protection Arrangements***,** London: Home Office.

Lipsky, M. (1980) *Street-Level Bureaucracy: Dilemmas of the Individual in Public Services*, New York: Russel Sage Foundation.

Loader, I. and Sparks, R. (2007) 'Contemporary landscapes of crime, order, and control: governance, risk and globalization', in M. Maguire, R. Morgan and R. Reiner (eds) *The Oxford Handbook of Criminology* (4th edition, pp 78-101), Oxford: Oxford University Press.

May, T. and Buck, M. (1998) 'Power, professionalism and organisational transformation', *Sociological Research Online*, vol 3, no 2, available at www.socresonline.org.uk/3/2/5.html

Ministry of Justice (2007) *MAPPA Guidance Version 2.0*, National Offender Management Service, London: Ministry of Justice.

Ministry of Justice (forthcoming: 2009) *Children and Young People: Annex to MAPPA Guidance*, London: Ministry of Justice.

Munro, E. (1996) 'Avoidable and unavoidable mistakes in child protection work', *British Journal of Social Work*, vol 26, no 6, pp 793-808.

Munro, E. (1998) 'Improving social workers' knowledge base in child protection work', *British Journal of Social Work*, vol 28, no 1, pp 89-105.

Nash, M. (2006) *Public Protection and the Criminal Justice Process*, Oxford: Oxford University Press.

Nash, M. (2007) 'Working with young people in a culture of public protection', in M. Blyth, E. Solomon and K. Baker (eds) *Young People and 'Risk'* (pp 85-95), Bristol: The Policy Press.

Northern Ireland Office (2008) *Draft Guidance on Public Protection Arrangements Northern Ireland: Consultation Document*, Belfast: Northern Ireland Office.

O'Malley, P. (2004) *Risk, Uncertainty and Government*, London: Cavendish Press/Glasshouse.

Page, E. and Jenkins, B. (2005) *Policy Bureaucracy: Government with a Cast of Thousands*, Oxford: Oxford University Press.

Parton, N. (2001) 'Risk and professional judgement', in L.-A. Cull and J. Roche (eds) *The Law and Social Work* (pp 61-70), Basingstoke: Palgrave.

Robinson, G. (2003) 'Technicality and indeterminacy in probation practice', *British Journal of Social Work*, vol 33, no 5, pp 593-610.

Rumgay, J. (2007) 'Partnerships in probation', in L. Gelsthorpe and R. Morgan (eds) *Handbook of Probation* (pp 542-64), Cullompton: Willan.

Sheppard, M. (1995) 'Social work, social science and practice wisdom', *British Journal of Social Work*, vol 25, no 3, pp 265-93.

Sheppard, M., Newstead, S., Di Caccavo, A. and Ryan, K. (2001) 'Comparative hypothesis assessment and quasi triangulation as process knowledge assessment strategies in social work practice', *British Journal of Social Work*, vol 31, no 6, pp 863-85.

Smith, R. (2007) *Youth Justice* (2nd edition), Cullompton: Willan.

Sutherland, A. and Jones, S. (2008) *MAPPA and Youth Justice: An Exploration of Youth Offending Team Engagement with Multi-Agency Public Protection Arrangements*, London: YJB.

Tata, C. (2002) 'So what does "and society" mean?', in C. Tata and N. Hutton (eds) *Sentencing and Society: International Perspectives* (pp 3-39), Aldershot: Ashgate.

Taylor, C. and White, S. (2006) 'Knowledge and reasoning in social work: educating for humane judgment', *British Journal of Social Work*, vol 36, no 6, pp 937-54.

Wood, J. and Kemshall, H. (2007) *The Operation and Experience of Multi-Agency Public Protection Arrangements*, Home Office Online Report 12/07, London: Home Office.

YJB (Youth Justice Board) (2006) *Multi-Agency Public Protection Arrangements: Guidance for Youth Offending Teams*, London: YJB.

Youth Justice Agency (2007) *Corporate and Business Plan 07/08*, Belfast: Youth Justice Agency.

MAPPA for kids: discourses of security, risk and children's rights

Noel Whitty[1]

Introduction

It is often claimed that, over the last decade, UK criminal justice policy has become increasingly preoccupied with the concepts of risk and public protection. Indeed, some academic and practitioner accounts now represent risk-based thinking and practices as the all-pervasive – and even dominant – force in contemporary offender management. However, during this very same period, the UK legal system[2] experienced its most seismic shift in decades: namely, the growth of rights consciousness and claims, the passing of the 1998 Human Rights Act (1998 HRA) and an ever-expanding culture of rights adjudication. This chapter will argue that these developments are significant and deserving of increased critical scrutiny. Of course, it may be the case that public perceptions, and media representations, of the relationship between risk and rights are skewed in only one direction – inevitable conflict – and, as with the 'war on terror', often with deeply problematic cultural, political and social effects (Mythen and Walklate, 2006). However, instead of always making such assumptions, my argument is that it is more fruitful to explore the actual nature – and effects of co-existence – of risk and rights discourses in contemporary criminal justice settings in the UK (Murphy and Whitty, 2007).

The focus of this book is the application of the Multi-Agency Public Protection Arrangements (MAPPA) framework within the youth justice system. A critical scrutiny of the risk–rights relationship in this context raises some distinct, and particularly troubling, questions. As evidenced by the title of this chapter ('MAPPA for kids'), one needs first to pause and ask: have the merits and costs of a policy of bringing children within a risk paradigm, which has been designed and generally functions with adult (male) offenders in mind, been adequately addressed (Kemshall, 2007; Nash, 2007)? This question is posed, not just because of the very different histories, cultures, practices and problems within youth and adult justice systems, but because it is possible to identify very distinctive associations between the status of *children* and the concepts of *risk* and *rights* respectively. In what follows, I focus on two of these: first, the role that risk plays in contemporary discourses around the child, and second, the impact of children's rights as protected by national and international law and practice. Thereafter I examine two contemporary debates – one on governance, the other on security.

Children and risk

Consider, first, the role that risk plays in contemporary discourses around children. There is the child at risk, the child who poses risks and the child who takes risks; and there are also overlaps between these. Official and public anxieties about each of these situations may often be genuine, socially desirable and progressive in outcome; yet, equally, such perceptions of risk may be harmful and often counterproductive in policy terms (Bell, 2002). One illustration of this double-edged nature of risk is the different constructions, and interpretations, placed on 'risky practices' in the context of teenage sexuality, contraception and pregnancy (Monk, 2007). Teenage risk management and risk taking may be viewed as pathological and aberrant behaviour, but they are also a key component in the physical, emotional and ethical development of individual or group identities (Mitchell et al, 2001). Therefore, if risk is increasingly to be correlated with youth *criminality*, it seems inevitable that 'youth' will be constructed in ever-deeper ways with notions of fear, dangerousness, deficiency and insecurity (Muncie, 2004). Indeed, it has been argued that 'relationships between adults and children are being fundamentally reconfigured as childhood itself is (re)constructed as being at risk' (James and James, 2008, p 8). My key preliminary point, therefore, is to raise questions about the capacity (and willingness) of youth justice personnel to recognise, and adequately respond to, the complexity and diversity of risk in young people's lives (see, for example, Batchelor, 2007) – if, as seems to be the case, the expanded use of MAPPA has been fully legitimised (YJB, 2007).

Children and rights

The second part of the distinctive association between children and the concepts of risk and rights relates to the universally recognised special status of *children's rights*. At the international level, instruments such as the 1989 United Nations (UN) Convention on the Rights of the Child and the 1985 UN Standard Minimum Rules for the Administration of Juvenile Justice ('Beijing Rules') have very significant normative influence. As Fortin (2005, pp 545-89) points out, the overall aim of the international human rights system in relation to young offenders is to ensure their just treatment, protection from harm, and diversion from imprisonment and punishment into care and rehabilitation. At the European level, the 1950 European Convention on Human Rights (ECHR) has generated an important children's rights jurisprudence (especially for young offenders) and, increasingly, the European Union has promoted the status of children in its laws and policies (McGlynn, 2006). At the national level, the 1989 and 2004 Children Acts are key mechanisms for giving specific effect to children's rights and needs (Masson, 2008). Furthermore, the 1998 HRA places a legal duty on all public authorities to act compatibly with ECHR rights, and potentially gives victims of rights violations new tools for political activism and legal redress.

This general outline of the enhanced legal status of children's rights in the UK must, however, be placed in context. On some indicators, such as those in the United Nations Children's Fund (UNICEF) report comparing the welfare of children in 21 Western states, the UK is ranked at the very bottom of the league (UNICEF, 2007; James and James, 2008). When the focus shifts to criminal justice policy in England and Wales, the landscape looks especially bleak. As many commentators have highlighted, the last 20 years have seen a dramatic move towards increasingly managerialist, populist and punitive policies for (potential) young offenders – for example, the expansion of new civil orders, risk-based intervention programmes and increased use of detention (see, generally, Muncie, 2004; Kemshall, 2007; Morgan and Newburn, 2007; Nash, 2007). Moreover, even where more positive attitudes and policies may be in evidence, practical reforms have been described as a 'strange blend of authoritarianism and liberalism' (Fortin, 2005, p 547; Newbury, 2008) and are increasingly focused on increasing the powers of a 'preventive-surveillance state' (Parton, 2008) –in relation to both 'feckless' and 'disruptive' children and their parents (Gillies, 2008).

Yet, while risk-based anxieties about youth crime now form a key part of 'law and order' politics, and risk has become an increasing preoccupation of the youth justice system, it does not inevitably follow that children's human rights norms and claims lose their significance. It is more accurate, I would argue, to describe the criminal justice landscape as one where both risk and rights discourses exist, intersect and sometimes clash. This is because human rights (law) serves both ideological and practical purposes. Rights retain a perennial appeal for individuals and groups because of their *potential* as tools of resistance, empowerment and emancipation (Goodale and Engle Merry, 2007). In the official ideology of the contemporary European nation state, human rights are also an important aspect of the legitimisation of governing power. Judicial self-identity, especially in the current House of Lords (and future UK Supreme Court), has become strongly associated with the creation of a rights-regarding UK constitutionalism (Dickson, 2006). New official bodies, such as the UK Joint Committee on Human Rights and the Equality and Human Rights Commission, have as their central remit the promotion and protection of human rights norms, and official human rights guidance for public authorities has been issued. More specifically, in relation to children in England and Wales, there is a long history of political activism by non-governmental organisations (NGOs) that, in recent years, have turned to human rights in order to protect individual rights and/or further reform strategies. The high-profile challenge to school uniform regulations in *Begum v Governors of Denbigh School* [2006] UKHL 15, while ultimately unsuccessful in the House of Lords, also attests to the new potential for a 'child' to invoke the 1998 HRA in order to challenge exercises of public authority power (Davies, 2006).

None of the above, it should be emphasised, is meant to be read as a prediction of any specific human rights victories for children. Judicial interpretation of rights is contingent and heavily contested, and general rights awareness and implementation throughout the public sector is dependent on a range of social, economic, political and legal factors (Halliday and Schmidt, 2004). Furthermore, the youth justice system is a distinct arena with particular legal and political cultures. My key argument here, however, is that the legal status of children's rights cannot just be ignored or discounted. Human rights need to be factored into accounts of the dominance, or otherwise, of risk-based policies and cultures (Murphy and Whitty, 2007).

Two key debates: governance and security

My argument so far has been directed towards highlighting the need for a critical analysis of the relationship between risk and children's rights discourses. In the remainder of this chapter, I want to problematise this relationship in a little more depth by engaging briefly with two distinct debates found in a variety of literatures. First, I want to draw attention to the governance of organisations in the criminal justice system, in particular the importance of the concept of 'organisational risk'. This is a different notion of risk to that discussed above and refers to the way that UK public administration is increasingly organised and regulated around risk-based concepts (Black, 2005; Hutter, 2006; Power, 2007). A range of internal and external actors now monitor how organisations create and manage their own 'business risk register'. This process is expected to identify the range of potential threats affecting an organisation, as well as the likelihood of their occurrence using different risk categories such as operational, financial, reputational or legal risks. What requires detailed analysis, I will argue, are the types of approaches being adopted (or not) by public authorities – such as the police, prison and probation services – in order to achieve compliance with both organisational risk-based obligations *and* human rights-based obligations.

The second debate of relevance that I want to highlight concerns security. Increasing emphases on (in)security and public protection – driven in part by the UK government's involvement in the 'war on terror' – have generated vociferous calls for a greater prioritisation of risks, even if this comes at the expense of established human rights norms (Goold and Lazarus, 2007). I will argue that, as war metaphors proliferate – war against drugs, crime, 'terror', 'feral kids' – and as (supposedly exceptional) counter-terrorism laws and discourses seep into everyday criminal justice contexts, current debates on security are a key terrain for the contestation of the relationship between risk and human rights.

Risk-based and rights-based governance

Regulation scholars have been to the fore in revealing the shift towards risk-based governance in both the public and the private sectors in the UK. Meanwhile, criminologists and criminal justice scholars have been to the fore in highlighting the shift towards individual risk assessment and management practices in the criminal justice system. And public and human rights lawyers have been to the fore in explaining the rights-based culture in the UK, and the legal obligations on public authorities under the 1998 HRA. There is, however, little research to date that combines all three perspectives. Yet, in order to make sense of the new landscape of risk-based youth justice, and in particular the operation of multi-agency frameworks like MAPPA and Youth Offending Teams (YOTs), a scholarship on 'risk and (children's) rights' is needed. A brief outline of some of the types of regulatory demands on criminal justice organisations should help to indicate how essential, and also how complex, constructing this scholarship will be in practice.

One example of the type of documentation and terminology now in use is the National Probation Service (2007) circular titled 'Risk management standard format'. This places the onus on managers to monitor their 'organisational risk' in the following terms:

> Organisations are increasingly being required to demonstrate effective corporate governance and internal control. At the same time there is also a primary objective to deliver performance. As we deal with risks on a daily basis, it is very important that the arrangements and processes for managing risk are well understood. For example the following types of action can be taken to respond to risk situation[s] on a daily basis: *Transfer some aspect of the risk; Tolerate the risk; Treat the risk; Terminate the risk.* All probation areas are expected to address risk issues because identifying the sources of risk and the area of impact on the business of the organisation will contribute to the effective management of the risk. (2007, p 2; emphasis in original)

The circular goes on to create a scale for identifying the likelihood of risks, ranging from 'very low' (less than 5% chance of occurrence) to 'very high' (more than 80% chance). It then provides guidance on assessing the impact of particular occurrences at different organisational levels under the headings of: *public protection* (exposing the public to injury or loss of life); *financial* (overspends from under £2 million to over £25 million); *reputation* (from public criticism up to ministerial resignation); and *delivery* (failure to achieve objectives). Templates of risk registers are also included in the circular, along with very basic notes on how to complete each section.

The crucial question is whether – and, if so, how – this general guidance to all 'business risk managers' in the probation service translates into day-to-day decisions and practices. In addition, questions about the sanctions for failure to comply (financial, political and/or legal); who actually has the final say on 'risky' decisions (civil servants, risk managers and/or lawyers); and what overall impact the prioritisation of organisational risk in managerial frameworks has on different criminal justice actors need to be tackled. On the evidence of some of the available literature, risk management is becoming the key indicator of service delivery and managerial performance for some actors (Genders and Player, 2007).

Allied with this new focus on *organisational* risk in the public sector, the functional roles of traditional criminal justice actors have also had to adapt to the increasing use of technologies of *individual* risk assessment and management. The Parole Board, for example, is required to undertake a risk assessment in every case that it considers (Shute, 2007). In the context of MAPPA, these different risk-based obligations operate to tie a range of organisations (parole boards, police forces, prison and probation services, housing authorities) into a network of risk compliance – in theory, if not always in practice (Whitty, 2007). Each organisation is expected both to satisfy a range of legal obligations to protect public safety and to comply with public sector governance rules to manage its own risk register. The performance of these tasks requires that notice is taken of both traditional legal rules (statutes, case law) and an increasingly diverse range of non-legal rules and standards (such as Treasury guidelines or Ministry of Justice circulars). The persistent emphasis in all this official documentation is on constant assessment, management and monitoring of the range of potential risks. The assumption, in each context, is that the relevant risk knowledge (actuarial, psychiatric, legal, financial) is both available and accurate. Effective risk management is also heavily linked with notions of defensibility: that is, always ensuring adequate lines of responsibility/blame in the event of undesirable outcomes.

Moving on from organisational risk, the second main type of regulatory demand that needs to be considered is the rights-based one. As outlined above, a variety of traditional legal sources, based on the common law, statutes and international treaties, are relevant to the protection of children's rights. In addition, children's rights norms are influenced by a range of non-legal, but authoritative, sources such as treaty body recommendations and NGO reports. Public sector regulatory obligations also derive from the demands, and standard setting, of a variety of audit, inspection and grievance-handling agencies and actors. Lastly, rights-based litigation (and the threat of it) is a regulatory influence both in the form of private law claims against public authorities (for example negligence) and public law actions (for example via judicial review). One might expect therefore that, for both normative and pragmatic reasons, the 1998 HRA would have a central influence on public sector thinking. Indeed, under the Act, all public authorities (and private companies who perform a 'public function') are subject to a direct legal obligation to respect ECHR rights in the performance of their duties (Lester and Pannick, 2004; Vincent-Jones, 2006). However, what this means in practice remains very unclear. The information that is available on public sector responses to the 1998 HRA portrays a mixed picture. It shows variable patterns of legal knowledge, political commitment, exercise of professional judgement, allocation of required resources and fear of sanction within public authorities (Clements and Thomas, 2005).

In the absence of more detailed research on the above questions of risk- and rights-based governance, any general observations must be tentative. However, in relation to the MAPPA framework, it can be argued that a focus on organisational risk management may be a key way for scholars and practitioners to understand its modes of operation. Admittedly, the diversity and hierarchy of MAPPA organisations and personnel means that identifying the exact nature of governing relationships will be a challenging task (Wood and Kemshall, 2007). At the same time, however, as Nash (2007, p 88) has argued, it is likely that the traditionally distinctive ethos and focus of each professional grouping within MAPPA may become increasingly blurred in light of the overall emphasis on public protection.

Another general point to be highlighted concerns the nature of risk in the criminal justice sector, and the salience of crime as a political topic. Hutter (2006, p 220), for example, has asked: despite all the official documentation and rhetoric surrounding internal and external audits of risk compliance, have government departments and public sector organisations actually bought into risk-based initiatives and, if so, to what extent? A case study of MAPPA might provide a particularly complex answer to this question, not least because the attempted management of organisational risks (such as public protection or ministerial reputation) can be closely connected to, and even determined by, the successful risk management of one individual offender. In other words, some criminal justice contexts may entwine organisational and individual risk practices more closely, and in more distinctive ways, than has been recognised to date.

Security: risk and the metaphor of (re)balancing

The second debate of relevance to a critical scholarship on MAPPA is the security one. War metaphors appear to be proliferating in public discourse about crime and punishment. Children have become a key target in some of these campaigns, with high-profile 'wars' being declared by politicians and some parts of the media on, variously, 'thugs', 'gangs', 'yobs', 'hoodies' and (in the Scottish context) 'neds'. Sparks (2006, pp 32-3) argues that the connections between 'different current mobilizations of fear, risk, and insecurity' are especially important. In particular, he calls for the exploration of:

> whatever relationship may exist between invocations of worry and concern about crime in its 'ordinary' or 'domestic' aspect (the crimes and incivilities of the street and neighbourhood, the usual stomping ground of criminologists) and those that have to do with the recent intensification of counter-terrorist activity and the controversies about the creation of new measures to deal with the sense of emergency that underpins this.

Clearly, both 'ordinary' and 'extraordinary' forms of crime generate huge pressures on political actors 'to demonstrate commitment, competence, and capacity' (for example through the extension of legal powers), and both 'have features in common on the level of cultural representation' (for example media coverage of public mistrust and fears). The end result, Sparks suggests, is to 'promote an elision between them in current discourse on "security"' (2006, p 33). I want to argue that this merging of the languages of crime control and warfare is of great significance for critical analyses of risk frameworks; in particular because of the new challenges it presents to advocates of human rights-based approaches to risk management.

In order to explain how current warfare debates are relevant to a context like MAPPA, I want to turn to how 'human rights' (and the 1998 HRA) have come to be stigmatised as contrary to public protection in the 'war on terror'. First, there have been numerous media and political claims that the 1998 HRA (and the potential threat of litigation) is generally a major distraction or obstacle undermining effective risk management – in particular, in relation to alleged sex offenders (Elliott, 2007; Whitty, 2007). Such zero-sum understandings of risk and rights have led to attacks on 'pro-rights' lawyers and judges for allegedly downplaying risks and endangering public safety. Second, while increased societal concerns with security/insecurity have been obvious for many years, including a shift towards increased privatisation of security (Zedner, 2003), it is the new national security context that has given heightened prominence to the relationship between risk and human rights. A discourse of 'new terrorism' has fuelled 'a generalized climate of fear and hostility', and made ever-more repressive legal responses appear socially acceptable (Mythen and Walklate, 2006, p 130; Dauvergne, 2007). In the US and the UK, notably, post-September 11 counter-terrorism strategies proclaim that the choice is clear – either prioritise risks or prioritise human rights:

> [S]ince 9/11 the words 'security' and 'human rights' have, in the collective imagination, now come to connote an almost insuperable opposition. Anyone who engages in the debate over security and human rights is almost immediately confronted by this dichotomy, tacit in the political call for a 'new balance' and explicit in newspaper editorials calling for the retreat from human rights. (Goold and Lazarus, 2007, p 1)

The reaction of human rights lawyers to this changed security landscape has been highly significant and is, I would argue, of general relevance for those engaging in debates on crime and risk reduction. Within human rights lawyers' responses, three trends can be identified: acknowledging the value of security; engaging more critically with the language and politics of risk; and focusing on legal knowledges of risk.

First, the value of human rights in times of (perceived) crisis has received renewed emphasis. However, this has gone hand in hand with a recognition of the need for human rights lawyers to more 'critically engage with the politics of security in late modern states' (Goold and Lazarus, 2007, p 7). Thus, recognising the importance of security as a value – and the ambivalence that the public and certain academic disciplines feel about some human rights discourses (Farmer, 2006; Loader, 2007) – entails confronting security-related claims in a direct and clear manner (Zedner, 2006;

Loader and Walker, 2007). Gearty (2008), for example, has been strongly critical of lawyers who have internalised the 'war on terror' assumptions of government officials, losing sight of both the relevance of historical and political context when analysing security threats, and the independent (and sceptical) role of the academic scholar. Others have highlighted the principled and empirical objections to the now-frequent resort to the imagery of 'balance' as a justification for curtailing human rights: the assumption of a 'hydraulic relationship between human rights safeguards and the promotion of security, that is that as one goes up the other must go down, and vice versa' (Ashworth, 2007, p 208; see also Zedner, 2005). As Ashworth (2007, p 208) argues, the adoption of such imagery 'trades on a cluster of associated terms – such as proportionality, reasonableness and fairness – that appear almost incontrovertible' (see also Goold et al, 2007).

The second trend emphasises that a critical focus on the language and politics of risk is now crucial. It is recognised that human rights scholarship in the past has not engaged sufficiently with risk, either at the theoretical level or in relation to the uses of risk assessment and management in legal contexts (Murphy and Whitty, 2007). Engaging with risk is most pressing in security contexts because risk discourses now generate, and reflect, perceptions of personal and public security – as well as providing the frame for governments to formulate, operate and evaluate their security policies (Zedner, 2006). In other words, risk-based beliefs and assumptions have the potential, if left unchallenged, to dominate debates on security not just because of the growing use of (apparently scientific) risk technologies, but also because of the *political* nature of conceptions of risk.

Third, human rights lawyers have argued for clear empirical evidence to be provided by those who seek to justify human rights limitations. That is, risk-based evidence of threats to public safety must be publicly disclosed – historically, this did not happen in national security contexts – and this evidence must be scrutinised according to identifiable legal norms. Risk technologies and expertise, in other words, must be brought under a direct human rights spotlight (Feldman, 2006). Judicial approaches towards risk have started to attract particular attention from human rights lawyers. Because of the nature of the new anti-terrorism legislation, with its emphasis on preventative detention and surveillance of suspected 'risky' individuals, a jurisprudence has begun to develop on reconciling the tension between risk management and human rights discourses (especially in relation to the legality and proportionality of restrictions such as control orders). A common feature of these academic critiques is a new emphasis on 'facing up to risk' and the argument that risk can be accommodated within, and reconciled with, human rights frameworks (Poole, 2008).

One major omission, however, in current human rights law scholarship is the lack of a sufficiently detailed focus on the *nature* of legal and scientific knowledges (Valverde, 2003). It is noteworthy, for example, that risk (assessment) tends to be thought of as an expert, rational or scientific knowledge, in contrast to human rights, which is generally seen as a values-based legal knowledge. Moreover, to date, appeals by human rights lawyers for more reliance to be placed on risk-based evidence, when assessing justifications for restricting rights, have tended to bypass the question of how that knowledge is constructed by practitioners. In my view, neither risk nor human rights should be defined as an impermeable or even as an internally coherent expert knowledge. In order to engage fully with risk frameworks, human rights lawyers need to recognise the ways in which political cultures influence both normative and scientific discourses. A critical awareness about who to use as an expert in (pre-)legal processes may also be in order (Good, 2007). Furthermore, there are distinctive methods, and effects, in play when *legal* actors and networks (courts, judges, lawyers) produce and circulate knowledges. In sum, then, the nature of risk knowledges, and rights knowledges, and their use and possible combinations cannot be left unexplored (Baker, 2007; Whitty, 2007; Ballucci, 2008).

To conclude this section, I want to return to the specific case of MAPPA and youth justice. A number of questions arise. First, in light of the aforementioned debates on security, how should one assess the policy decision to bring children within the MAPPA framework? On one reading, it is easy in the current climate to see how particular young offenders can be seen as so 'risky' that they should be represented, and treated, as 'mini adults'. The aura of risk expertise, and alleged risk prioritisation, surrounding MAPPA may also make the inclusion of children particularly politically compelling. However, it may be that, instead of a calculated strategy of increased regulation and coercion, this is an example of the type of drift or spillover that one sometimes sees in the criminal justice system; whereby structures and powers are put in place for one purpose, but are gradually extended to another (as in the case of the morphing of Anti-Social Behaviour Orders [ASBOs] into the new control orders for alleged terrorist suspects).

Second, it was argued above that risk-based beliefs and assumptions have the potential, if left unchallenged, to dominate public debates on security. One counter to this has been the invocation of the normative power of (adults') human rights. Admittedly, in certain contexts, this has been a failure because of the investment people now have in a heightened sense of security and the perception of offenders as 'undeserving' rights-holders. It is, however, worth speculating on the potential, and likely success, of a *children's rights* discourse. Unfortunately, in light of the continued political distaste for the concept of children's rights generally and the emotive reactions to contemporary youth crime and offenders, one must remain pessimistic (Hope and Sparks, 2000; Nash, 2007). Yet, if every conflict involving children is to be reconceptualised as an issue of 'security' – including, for example, anxieties about daily interactions among pupils in schools – then it needs to be recognised that this will come at a very great cost. As Sparks (2006, p 47) has asked, 'What kind of people are we being encouraged to be by these discourses?'. A children's rights approach surely offers the potential, at the very least, for promoting alternative visions of risk, security and society.

Conclusion

The aim of this chapter has been to provide a critical perspective on the application of the MAPPA framework within the youth justice system. In calling for scrutiny of the relationship between risk and (children's) rights, I have sought to draw attention to the complexity and diversity of risk in children's lives, as well as to the consequences of the increasing correlations being drawn between risk, (youth) criminality and security. 'Is MAPPA for kids?' is a question that, to my mind, is not being sufficiently debated at present. In light of the obvious costs of bringing children within an adult framework dominated by a focus on public protection, the absence of a robust debate on this question should be a cause for particular concern. In addition to the need for an increased focus on risk assessment and management of (potential) individual offenders, I have argued that there is also a need for critical scrutiny of how criminal justice actors, in light of their involvement in MAPPA, are defining and managing their organisational risks.

The second main theme of this chapter concerned the need to take account of the significance of children's rights in national and international law and practice. Especially in light of the 1998 HRA, the status of human rights now has a heightened recognition within the UK, and a range of legal obligations apply to public authorities in relation to protecting children's rights. I have argued that the relevance and potential of human rights must not be discounted even if serious concerns have been expressed, especially in the criminal justice context, about rights protection in practice (UK Children's Commissioners, 2008). Instead of accounts of the dominance of risk-based policies and cultures, it would be more apposite – and strategically more useful – to start investigating the ways in which risk and rights discourses exist, intersect and compete for dominance.

Notes

[1] My thanks to Thérèse Murphy and the editors for their comments.

[2] It is important to recognise the distinctive nature of the UK legal and political system as a whole and, since the three devolution Acts of 1998, also that of Scotland, Northern Ireland and Wales.

References

Ashworth, A. (2007) 'Security, terrorism and the value of human rights', in B. Goold and L. Lazarus (eds) *Security and Human Rights* (pp 203-26), Oxford: Hart Publishing.

Baker, K. (2007) 'Risk in practice: systems and practitioner judgement', in M. Blyth, E. Solomon and K. Baker (eds) *Young People and 'Risk'* (pp 25-38), Bristol: The Policy Press.

Ballucci, D. (2008) 'Risk in action: the practical effects of the Youth Management Assessment', *Social and Legal Studies*, vol 17, no 2, pp 175-97.

Batchelor, S. (2007) '"Getting mad wi' it": risk seeking by young women', in K. Hannah-Moffat and P. O'Malley (eds) *Gendered Risks* (pp 205-28), London: Routledge-Cavendish.

Bell, V. (2002) 'The vigilant(e) parent and the paedophile', *Feminist Theory*, vol 3, no 1, pp 83-102.

Black, J. (2005) 'The emergence of risk-based regulation and the new public risk management in the United Kingdom', *Public Law*, pp 512-48.

Clements, L. and Thomas, P. (eds) (2005) *Human Rights Act: A Success Story?*, London: Blackwell.

Dauvergne, C. (2007) 'Security and migration law in the less brave new world', *Social and Legal Studies*, vol 16, no 4, pp 533-49.

Davies, G. (2006) '(Not yet) taking rights seriously: the House of Lords in *Begum* v. *Headteacher and Governors of Denbigh High School*, on religious clothing in schools', 13 November, SSRN, http://ssrn.com/abstract=945319

Dickson, B. (2006) 'Safe in their hands: the Law Lords and human rights', *Legal Studies*, vol 26, no 3, pp 329-46.

Elliot, M. (2007) 'The Parole Board and the changing face of public law', in N. Padfield (ed) *Who to Release? Parole, Fairness and Criminal Justice* (pp 43-62), Cullompton: Willan.

Farmer, L. (2006) 'Tony Martin and the nightbreakers: criminal law, victims and the power to punish', in S. Armstrong and L. McAra (eds) *Perspectives on Punishment: The Contours of Control* (pp 49-67), Oxford: Oxford University Press.

Feldman, D. (2006) 'Human rights, terrorism and risk: the role of politicians and judges', *Public Law*, pp 364-84.

Fortin, J. (2005) *Children's Rights and the Developing Law*, Cambridge: Cambridge University Press.

Gearty, C. (2008) 'The superpatriotic fervour of the moment', *Oxford Journal of Legal Studies*, vol 28, no 1, pp 183-200.

Genders, E. and Player, E. (2007) 'The commercial context of criminal justice: prison privatisation and the perversion of purpose', *Criminal Law Review*, pp 513-29.

Gillies, V. (2008) 'Perspectives on parenting responsibility: contextualizing values and practices', *Journal of Law and Society*, vol 35, no 1, pp 95-112.

Good, A. (2007) *Anthropology and Expertise in the Asylum Courts*, London: Glasshouse.

Goodale, M. and Engle Merry, S. (eds) (2007) *The Practice of Human Rights: Tracking Law Between the Global and Local*, Cambridge: Cambridge University Press.

Goold, B. and Lazarus, L. (eds) (2007) *Security and Human Rights*, Oxford: Hart Publishing.

Goold, B., Lazarus, L. and Swiney, G. (2007) *Public Protection, Proportionality, and the Search for Balance*, London: Ministry of Justice.

Halliday, S. and Schmidt, P. (eds) (2004) *Human Rights Brought Home: Socio-Legal Perspectives on Human Rights in the National Context*, Oxford: Hart Publishing.

Hope, T. and Sparks, R. (eds) (2000) *Crime, Risk and Insecurity*, London: Routledge.

Hutter, B. (2006) 'Risk, regulation and management', in P. Taylor-Gooby and J. Zinn (eds) *Risk in Social Science* (pp 202-27), Oxford: Oxford University Press.

James, A. and James, A. (2008) 'European childhoods: an overview', in A. James and A. James (eds) *European Childhoods* (pp 1-13), Basingstoke: Palgrave Macmillan.

Kemshall, H. (2007) 'Risk assessment and risk management: the right approach?', in M. Blyth, E. Solomon and K. Baker (eds) *Young People and 'Risk'* (pp 7-23), Bristol: The Policy Press.

Lester, A. and Pannick, D. (2004) *Human Rights Law and Practice*, London: LexisNexis.

Loader, I. (2007) 'The cultural lives of security and rights', in B. Goold and L. Lazarus (eds) *Security and Human Rights* (pp 27-43), Oxford: Hart Publishing.

Loader, I. and Walker, N. (2007) *Civilizing Security*, Cambridge: Cambridge University Press.

McGlynn, C. (2006) *Families and the European Union*, Cambridge: Cambridge University Press.

Masson, J. (2008) 'The state as parent: the reluctant parent? The problems of parents as last resort', *Journal of Law and Society*, vol 35, no 1, pp 52-74.

Mitchell, W., Crawshaw, P., Bunton, R. and Green, E. (2001) 'Situating young people's experiences of risk and identity', *Health, Risk and Society*, vol 3, no 2, pp 217-33.

Monk, D. (2007) 'Teenage pregnancies and sex education: constructing the girl/ woman subject', in V. Munro and C. Stychin (eds) *Sexuality and the Law: Feminist Engagements* (pp 201-22), London: Glasshouse Press.

Morgan, R. and Newburn, T. (2007) 'Youth justice', in M. Maguire, R. Morgan and R. Reiner (eds) *The Oxford Handbook of Criminology* (4th edition, pp 1024-60), Oxford: Oxford University Press.

Muncie, J. (2004) *Youth and Crime*, London: Sage Publications.

Murphy, T. and Whitty, N. (2007) 'Risk and human rights in UK prison governance', *British Journal of Criminology*, vol 47, no 5, p 798-816.

Mythen, G. and Walklate, S. (2006) 'Communicating the terrorist risk: harnessing a culture of fear?', *Crime, Media, Culture*, vol 2, no 2, pp 123-42.

Nash, M. (2007) 'Working with young people in a culture of public protection', in M. Blyth, E. Solomon and K. Baker (eds) *Young People and 'Risk'* (pp 85-95), Bristol: The Policy Press.

National Probation Service (2007) 'Risk management standard format', Circular PC02, London: NOMS.

Newbury, A. (2008) 'Youth crime: whose responsibility?', *Journal of Law and Society*, vol 35, no 1, pp 131-49.

Parton, N. (2008) 'The "Change for Children" Programme in England: towards the "preventive-surveillance state"', *Journal of Law and Society*, vol 35, no 1, pp 166-87.

Poole, T. (2008) 'Courts and conditions of uncertainty in "times of crisis"', *Public Law*, pp 234-59.

Power, M. (2007) *Organized Uncertainty*, Oxford: Oxford University Press.

Shute, S. (2007) 'Parole and risk assessment', in N. Padfield (ed) *Who to Release? Parole, Fairness and Criminal Justice* (pp 21-42), Cullompton: Willan.

Sparks, R. (2006) 'Ordinary anxieties and states of emergency: statecraft and spectatorship in the new politics of insecurity', in S. Armstrong and L. McAra (eds) *Perspectives on Punishment: The Contours of Control* (pp 31-47), Oxford: Oxford University Press.

UK Children's Commissioners for England (2008) *Report to the UN Committee on the Rights of the Child*, London: The Stationery Office, www.11million.org.uk

UNICEF (United Nations Children's Fund) (2007) *Child Poverty in Perspective: An Overview of Child Wellbeing in Rich Countries*, Florence: Innocenti Research Centre.

Valverde, M. (2003) *Law's Dream of a Common Knowledge*, Princeton, NJ: Princeton University Press.

Vincent-Jones, P. (2006) *The New Public Contracting*, Oxford: Oxford University Press.

Whitty, N. (2007) 'Risk, human rights and the management of a serious sex offender', *Zeitschrift für Rechtssoziologie*, vol 28, no 2, pp 265-76.

Wood, J. and Kemshall, H. (2007) *The Operation and Experience of Multi-Agency Protection Arrangements (MAPPA)*, London: Home Office.

YJB (Youth Justice Board) (2007) *Risk Management Policies of Youth Offending Teams*, London: YJB.

Zedner, L. (2003) 'Too much security?', *International Journal of the Sociology of Law*, vol 31, no 3, pp 155-84.

Zedner, L. (2005) 'Securing liberty in the face of terror: reflections from criminal justice', *Journal of Law and Society*, vol 32, no 4, pp 507-33.

Zedner, L. (2006) 'Neither safe nor sound? The perils and possibilities of risk', *Canadian Journal of Criminology and Criminal Justice*, vol 48, no 3, pp 423-34.

Conclusion

Kerry Baker and Alex Sutherland

'Is MAPPA for kids?' (Whitty, this volume). Why, when Multi-Agency Public Protection Arrangements (MAPPA) are now an established and seemingly accepted part of the criminal justice system, does this question need to be asked? In fact, why devote a book to a rather specialist area of practice that only directly affects a small number of young people? Because, as the contributors to this volume have shown, debates about MAPPA require, and can also be a catalyst for, consideration of a range of significant theoretical and practical issues, including concepts of risk; the role of children's rights; professional decision making; organisational culture; partnership working; and offender rehabilitation, to name just some. To conclude, therefore, this chapter brings together key themes, highlights gaps in our current knowledge and puts forward suggestions for the future development and application of MAPPA to young people.

Key issues

Notwithstanding the historical accounts of the development of MAPPA (Bryan and Doyle, 2003) and various research studies that have looked at the practical workings of these arrangements (Maguire et al, 2001; Kemshall et al, 2005), it remains unclear as to whether incorporating young people within MAPPA was a deliberate choice as part of the government's pursuit of the public protection agenda or whether it was an example of policy drift (Whitty, this volume). If the former, then there are questions as to why it was thought appropriate to include young people into a system designed initially for adult sex offenders and if the latter, then it is surely problematic if this happened almost accidentally.

Either way, the fact that the reforms in youth justice and the development of MAPPA occurred over the same time period, but essentially separately from each other, helps to explain why the inclusion of young people within MAPPA is sometimes difficult. Research shows a somewhat patchy picture with regard to the operation of MAPPA in youth justice due to a considerable degree of variation in the extent, quality and type of interaction between Youth Offending Teams (YOTs) and MAPPA (Sutherland and Jones, 2008). The current estimate of 2,000 young people subject to MAPPA in England and Wales is an approximation and more reliable data are needed. This should include breakdowns by age, gender, ethnicity and offence type so that we have a better understanding of which young people are being drawn into this particular aspect of contemporary risk penality.

At a practical level, the benefits of MAPPA for young people include their potential to challenge insular thinking and thus promote more rigorous assessments (Kemshall and Wood, this volume; Sutherland, this volume), to enable shared responsibility for defensible decision making and to facilitate access to additional services that can help to manage and/or reduce risk. On the other hand, concerns have been expressed about the quasi-legal nature of MAPPA (McNeill, this volume), their potential for net widening and stigmatising, and whether they really add anything to the risk management of young people given that YOTs are already multi-agency organisations (Sutherland, this volume).

Any evaluation of MAPPA thus needs to take account of both their potential advantages and disadvantages. While this book has focused on analysing the operation of MAPPA in England and Wales, it will in future be essential to look at the UK as a whole and consider the lessons to be learned from the introduction of MAPPA in Scotland and Northern Ireland. The implementation of similar models of MAPPA but within different legislative, organisational and social contexts may well trigger new debates, which, in turn, could help to sharpen our understanding of how to work with young people.

Knowledge and theory

Our understanding of how MAPPA work has improved as research studies have thrown light on recent practice (Kemshall et al, 2005; Wood and Kemshall, 2007; Sutherland and Jones, 2008). However, one obvious gap that needs to be addressed as a priority is to explore young people's views about their experiences of being subject to MAPPA as their voice is almost entirely absent from this debate. One might expect to find some resentment of the additional restrictions that MAPPA involvement might trigger, although perhaps there might also be parallels with young people's views of the surveillance elements of Intensive Supervision and Surveillance Programmes (ISSPs) (such as tagging), which some found helpful as it provided a credible excuse to help them resist peer pressure (Moore et al, 2004). This is all rather speculative but we will not know until young people are asked. Also lacking from the literature is any substantive analysis of the role of children's services in relation to young people subject to MAPPA.[1] It would be useful to know more about factors such as their attendance at MAPP meetings, their understanding of risk management and the resources that children's services are able to contribute for young people.

With regard to risk assessment and risk management, MAPPA professionals are charged with the difficult task of determining 'the nature and degree of risk a given individual may pose for certain kinds of behaviours, in light of anticipated conditions and contexts' (Borum, 2000, p 1264). Despite developments in risk assessment frameworks and the gradually expanding range of programmes and interventions, there are still significant gaps, particularly in relation to understanding violent behaviour by young people (Burman et al, 2008; McNeill, this volume). Two ideas to consider in relation to furthering knowledge in this area would be the literature on situational theories of behaviour and the distinction between 'stable' and 'acute' risk factors. These are not, of course, the only avenues to explore, and there is no space here for anything other than a cursory discussion, but these could be two interesting options. Collins (2008, p 1), for example, argues that looking at the 'dynamics of situations' should be at the heart of attempts to understand violence rather than focusing on the characteristics of individuals (see also Wikström, 2006). The 'stable and acute' model of risk assessment emphasises the distinction between the long-term factors underlying behaviour ('stable') and the more immediate circumstantial triggers ('acute') and argues for the importance of the latter in effective day-to-day risk management (Hanson and Harris, 2000). As yet, it is not clear how well a model developed for adult sex offenders could be applied to young people. Assessment tools for young people such as *Asset* or the Structured Assessment of Violence Risk in Youth (SAVRY) (Borum et al, 2003) already acknowledge the distinction between types of risk factors to some extent but perhaps need to do so more.

Each chapter in this book has raised questions about the concept of 'risk' and its application in criminal justice settings. First, risk is not the only, nor necessarily the predominant, practice paradigm and in the mélange of different theoretical perspectives and approaches to offender management 'we should not expect "risk" to emerge pristine and unadulterated from the encounter' (Loader and Sparks, 2007, p 85). This can be seen even in something as seemingly risk focused as MAPPA – the discussions here have shown that concerns about welfare and rights continue to influence systems and specific decisions. Whitty's call in this volume for a 'scholarship on risk and children's rights' to look at the intersection between these different discourses is of particular importance and, if taken up, could be critical in helping 'to make sense of the new landscape of risk-based youth justice'.

Second, the link between management of organisational risks and management of risks posed by individual offenders is one that warrants further consideration and MAPPA may be a particularly rich example to study. Third, there is a need to move away from overly simplistic assumptions that risk-based ways of working must necessarily be punitive or incapacitatory and instead to recognise that this is a term that can encompass both exclusionary and inclusive practices (O'Malley, 2004; Baker, this volume). Little is currently known about the details of interventions or MAPPA risk management plans for young people, but further information on this would contribute to a more nuanced debate about risk management. Fourth, the growing interest in developmental and ecological approaches to offender rehabilitation suggests that 'targeting risk may be a *necessary* but not a *sufficient* condition for reducing reoffending' (McNeill, this volume). Thus, just as at the macro level, risk has to be viewed alongside other paradigms, so at the micro level of interventions with individual offenders, a focus on risk may need to be supplemented with other approaches to promoting desistance.

Policy and practice

Moving on to think about the more practical issues of policy and practice, one obvious area of concern is around multi-agency cooperation and partnerships. It is in the longer-term interests of adult services to work with youth justice organisations to identify and reduce risk before young people transfer to the probation service or to adult prisons. One might perhaps draw an analogy with the education system in that the performance and achievements of secondary schools are to some extent dependent on the intake from feeder schools. Similarly, the task facing practitioners in adult criminal justice services will be influenced by how effective the interventions provided by youth justice colleagues have been. Viewed from this perspective, it is perhaps somewhat surprising to see the evidence of difficulties with, and sometimes lack of, interaction between YOTs and MAPPA (Kemshall et al, 2005; Sutherland and Jones, 2008).

Some of the reasons for this have been explored in this volume (Sutherland, this volume), with a particular focus on organisational culture and tension. The contested nature of youth justice (Eadie and Canton, 2002) and the expectation that YOTs should link effectively with criminal justice services on one side and children's services on the other (YJB, 2004) perhaps help to explain why MAPPA participants from adult-based agencies with more tightly defined corporate structures and goals may not find it easy to engage with YOTs or young people. In considering how to remedy this, one issue emerging from the literature surrounds the need for greater clarity about what partnerships are for (Rumgay, 2007). Partnerships can have a number of purposes, for example to facilitate information sharing, to pool resources, to spread reputational risk or to improve accountability and monitoring. All of these may be laudable but clear rationales are needed if YOTs – who already enjoy many of the benefits of multi-agency working – are to see that there will be a benefit in return for the time and resources they invest in MAPPA.

A second theme in relation to policy implementation concerns localism. For example, while there has recently been some central government recognition of the need for the specific needs of young people in MAPPA to be taken into account (Ministry of Justice, forthcoming), the extent to which any of this is reflected in day-to-day practice will depend on MAPPA coordinators and chairs, on the quality of relationships and on local organisational cultures. A further example is around variations in the thresholds and criteria for deciding who requires risk management at MAPPA levels 2 and 3 (Kemshall and Wood, this volume; Sutherland, this volume). Some of this could be attributable to practical issues such as areas having different referral forms although it is likely that the introduction of new standardised documentation will reduce the impact of this kind of procedural variance. Some of the variation is also likely to be caused by differences in the local 'risk context' (Sutherland, this volume), however, and this illustrates the tension between the goal of having consistency in policy implementation across the country and the desire to have services that are locally responsive and accountable. There are no easy answers to this dilemma although the much-cited principle of defensible decision making perhaps offers one way to manage this if variance in practice can be justified on the basis of rigorous decision making that takes full account of specific local factors.

This leads into a third policy and practice-related theme about the use of professional discretion. Baker (this volume) highlighted the need to recognise diverse types of discretion and also how the balance between rules and discretion varies at different stages in the MAPPA process. It is therefore not possible simply to say that practitioners need more or less discretion in an 'all-or-nothing' way, but rather we need to consider whether there should be more freedom at some points and less in others. In particular, the need for all young people meeting the eligibility criteria to be notified to MAPPA should be reconsidered and consideration given to adopting the approach to be implemented in Northern Ireland of saying that young people do not need to be notified to MAPPA if ordinary agency management is adequate (level 1) but that practitioners have the discretion to refer cases if additional multi-agency input at levels 2 or 3 would be beneficial.[2]

The problem in England and Wales is whether staff are sufficiently skilled to do this, given concerns about the quality of assessment practice (Baker, 2007). Improving practice is therefore critical as there is little chance of politicians or policy makers giving practitioners more discretion until there is increased confidence in their ability to manage potentially high-risk young people effectively. It is not at all clear, however, to what extent current initiatives for developing the skills and qualifications of the youth justice workforce (Monk, this volume) will have an impact in terms of promoting knowledge in this specific area of dealing with the most serious offenders, and this must be a cause for concern.

Fourth, listening to young people's views raises some interesting questions about risk management as Kemshall and Wood (this volume) highlight in their discussion of how young people perceive and negotiate risk. For example, if they rationalise their own risk-taking behaviour then it becomes more difficult for MAPPA to create risk management plans that young people will 'own' and comply with. The Good Lives Model (GLM), with its focus on primary human goods as sources of motivation, has been identified as something that could perhaps provide a more appropriate framework for working with young people than exclusively risk-based methods (McNeill, this volume; Ward and Maruna, 2007). While this is certainly a promising model, it needs to be viewed alongside evidence suggesting that some young people who offend are fatalistic about the future (Kemshall and Wood, this volume) and hence may not want, or may find it difficult, to work with such an approach. This is not to say that such models should not be considered – far from it – but rather to suggest that taking young people's views seriously requires us to think further about their application.

Symbolism, morality and politics

'We select the risks that we want to calculate and manage in large measure because of the ways in which they alarm and disconcert us' (Loader and Sparks, 2007, p 94). Current public concern over gangs and the use of weapons by young people, fuelled by the media and reinforced by a reactionary political agenda, is one obvious element of wider societal concern about, and fear of, youth crime. In prioritising the risk management of violent and sexual offenders – in contrast, say, to employers who breach health and safety regulations in the workplace resulting in death or injury to staff (Bottoms, 1977; Tombs and Whyte, 2008) – MAPPA have significant symbolic power. Whitty (this volume) highlights the power of metaphors used in security discourse and how they seep into general perceptions of 'ordinary' crime. One might also suggest that, in a more specific way, the risk language of MAPPA permeates into other aspects of criminal justice services – including youth justice – and thus has an effect that is much wider than the direct impact on specific offenders.

Discussions about MAPPA should never simply be about procedures but need to recognise the moral issues involved, for example the importance of protecting citizens, upholding the law, caring for children (including those who offend) and allowing people to make choices as moral agents. All of these intersect in the operation of MAPPA. Risk management is not just a technical activity but also a moral one, an obvious point perhaps but one that can often be forgotten among the procedural labyrinth. Zedner (2007, p 262) argues that we should be concerned when '[r]esponding to crime as a moral wrong becomes secondary to estimating, calculating, preventing, and minimising losses and insuring against them'. One of the criticisms of the Risk-Needs-Responsivity (RNR) model of rehabilitation and risk management, for example, is that it is 'vague about values and core principles … hence its moral basis is underdeveloped' (McNeill, this volume, citing Ward and Maruna, 2007). There is a need, therefore, to ensure that developments around MAPPA acknowledge the moral issues involved and, even though there will inevitably be differences of opinion about policy, are transparent about the choices that have been made and the reasons for so doing.

Risk management is also a political matter. It has been argued that '[w]e are not a "risk society" in the sense of being exposed to more, or more serious dangers. If we are a risk society it is because we have come to be more conscious of the risks that we run and more intensely engaged in attempts to measure and manage them' (Garland, 2003, p 71). The quantity of criminal justice legislation in recent years bears witness to this activism on the part of government and MAPPA are just one of many possible examples of initiatives aimed at measuring and managing risk.

It is common to suggest that much of this is driven by popular and media panic but there is also a sense in which the criminal justice system can be used to moderate public demands for vengeance and/or exclusionary measures. MAPPA present an interesting case in point here. For example, in the face of media demands for greater access to information about sex offenders (Nash, 2006), allowing controlled disclosure of relevant information through MAPPA (Ministry of Justice, 2007) can be seen as a way of limiting the impact of penal populism (Pratt, 2006; Kemshall, 2008). MAPPA guidance (Ministry of Justice, 2007) clearly advocates a parsimonious approach in which cases are managed at the lowest level that is compatible with a defensible assessment of risk. Whether such an approach can be sustained in the face of current fears over crime and public expectations that government should be seen to be 'doing something' is currently unknown but will ultimately depend on political choices and priorities.

Finally, we return to the question of the intersection of risk, welfare and rights in youth justice. This is also a political decision, as evidenced by the fact that other jurisdictions prioritise these elements in ways that differ markedly from the current approach in England and Wales (Hill et al, 2007). It is beyond the scope of this book to provide any detailed suggestions for how these factors should interact except to say that it is not a zero-sum game and each needs to be reflected in the workings of MAPPA.

And so....

We return to the question 'Is MAPPA for kids?'. MAPPA can operate as part of a measured response to public demands for punitive responses to offending and, as such, may have benefits for young people if they help to ensure that interventions are appropriate and that information is shared in a controlled way. However, there is still a sense in which young people are regarded as an 'afterthought' within MAPPA and, despite pockets of good practice, the involvement of YOTs in MAPPA remains difficult in many ways. More attention needs to be given to the intersection between risk and rights discourses, to the coordination of MAPPA and Local Safeguarding Children Board (LSCB) activity, and to the exercise of professional discretion by suitably skilled staff if MAPPA are to work more effectively for young people. We hope that the ideas and discussions presented here will stimulate some much-needed critical debate to inform the development of future policy and practice.

Notes
[1] As distinct from their role in relation to child protection in cases involving adult offenders who present a risk to children.

[2] This could also reduce the practical problems likely to ensue if MAPPA become overloaded with level 1 cases. As one symposium participant pointed out, 'all the work of MAPPA coordinators right around the country is clogged up with a whole series of in a sense artificially constructed groups of people that you have to consider ... many of whom you then immediately filter out because they're not currently dangerous'.

References

Baker, K. (2007) 'Risk, uncertainty and public protection: assessment of young people who offend', *British Journal of Social Work*, doi: 10.1093/bjsw/bcm054

Borum, R. (2000) 'Assessing violence risk among youth', *Journal of Clinical Psychology*, vol 56, no 10, pp 1263-88.

Borum, R., Bartel, P. and Forth, A.E. (2003) *Manual for the Structured Assessment for Violence Risk in Youth (SAVRY) Version 1.1*, Tampa, FL: University of South Florida.

Bottoms, A. (1977) 'Reflections on the renaissance of dangerousness', *The Howard Journal*, vol 16, no 2, pp 70-96.

Bryan, T. and Doyle, P. (2003) 'Developing Multi-Agency Public Protection Arrangements', in A. Matravers (ed) *Sex Offenders in the Community: Managing and Reducing the Risks* (pp 189-206), Cullompton: Willan.

Burman, M., Armstrong, S., Batchelor, S., McNeill, F. and Nicholson, J. (2008) *Research and Practice in Risk Assessment and Risk Management of Children and Young People Engaging in Offending Behaviours*, Paisley: Risk Management Authority, available from www.rmascotland.gov.uk/

Collins, R. (2008) *Violence: A Micro-Sociological Theory*, Princeton, NJ: Princeton University Press.

Eadie, T. and Canton, R. (2002) 'Practising in a context of ambivalence: the challenge for youth justice workers', *Youth Justice*, vol 2, no 1, pp 14-26.

Garland, D. (2003) 'The rise of risk', in R. Ericson and A. Doyle (eds) *Risk and Morality* (pp 48-86), London: University of Toronto Press.

Hanson, R. and Harris, A. (2000) 'Where should we intervene? Dynamic predictors of sexual offense recidivism', *Criminal Justice & Behavior*, vol 27, no 1, pp 6-35.

Hill, M., Lockyer, A. and Stone, F. (2007) *Youth Justice and Child Protection*, London: Jessica Kingsley Publishers.

Kemshall, H. (2008) 'Rationalities of risk in crime and prevention: an overview', paper presented at the 1st International Sociological Association Forum of Sociology, Barcelona, Spain, 5-8 September.

Kemshall, H., Mackenzie, G., Wood, J., Bailey, R. and Yates, J. (2005) *Strengthening Multi-Agency Public Protection Arrangements*, London: Home Office.

Loader, I. and Sparks, R. (2007) 'Contemporary landscapes of crime, order, and control: governance, risk and globalization', in M. Maguire, R. Morgan and R. Reiner (eds) *The Oxford Handbook of Criminology* (4th edition), Oxford: Oxford University Press.

Maguire, M., Kemshall, H., Noaks, L. and Wincup, E. (2001) *Risk Management of Sexual and Violent Offenders: The Work of Public Protection Panels*, Police Research Series No 139, London: Home Office.

Ministry of Justice (2007) *MAPPA Guidance Version 2.0*, National Offender Management Service, London: Ministry of Justice.

Ministry of Justice (forthcoming: 2009) *Children and Young People: Annex to MAPPA Guidance*, London: Ministry of Justice.

Moore, R., Gray, E., Roberts, C., Merrington, S., Waters, I., Fernandez, R., Hayward, G. and Rogers, R.D. et al (2004) *National Evaluation of the Intensive Supervision and Surveillance Programme: Interim Report to the Youth Justice Board*, London: YJB.

Nash, M. (2006) *Public Protection and the Criminal Justice Process*, Oxford: Oxford University Press.

O'Malley, P. (2004) *Risk, Uncertainty and Government*, London: Cavendish Press/ Glasshouse.

Pratt, J. (2006) *Penal Populism (Key Ideas in Criminology)*, London: Routledge.

Rumgay, J. (2007) 'Partnerships in probation', in L. Gelsthorpe and R. Morgan (eds) *Handbook of Probation*, Cullompton: Willan.

Sutherland, A. and Jones, S. (2008) *MAPPA and Youth Justice: An Exploration of Youth Offending Team Engagement with Multi-Agency Public Protection Arrangements*, London: YJB.

Tombs, S. and Whyte, D. (2008) *A Crisis of Enforcement: The Decriminalisation of Death and Injury at Work*, London: Centre for Crime and Justice Studies.

Ward, T. and Maruna, S. (2007) *Rehabilitation: Beyond the Risk Paradigm*, London: Routledge.

Wikström, P.-O. (2006) 'Individuals, settings and acts of crime: situational mechanisms and the explanation of crime', in P.-O. Wikström and R. Sampson (eds) *The Explanation of Crime: Context, Mechanisms and Development* (pp 61-107), Cambridge: Cambridge University Press.

Wood, J. and Kemshall, H. (2007) *The Operation and Experience of Multi-Agency Public Protection Arrangements*, Home Office Online Report No 12/07, London: Home Office.

YJB (Youth Justice Board) (2004) *Sustaining the Success*, London: YJB.

Zedner, L. (2007) 'Seeking security by eroding rights: the side-stepping of due process', in B. Goold and L. Lazarus (eds) *Security and Human Rights* (pp 257-75), Oxford: Hart Publishing.

Appendix: Qualifying offences for MAPPA categories 1 and 2

This appendix sets out the offences which currently meet the eligibility criteria for MAPPA categories 1 and 2 (see chapter one, page 17).[1]

Relevant sexual offences (MAPPA category 1)

These are the thresholds that must be met before an offender becomes subject to the notification requirements of Part 2 of the 2003 Sexual Offences Act (and thereby becomes a MAPPA category 1 case).

Indecent photographs of children under 16 (1978 Protection of Children Act, Section 1)

Where the offender is under 18: 12 months' imprisonment

Where the offender is 18 or above: automatic registration

Importing indecent photographs of children under 16 (1979 Customs and Excise Management Act, Section 170 and 1876 Customs Consolidation Act, Section 42)

Where the offender is under 18: 12 months' imprisonment

Where the offender is 18 or above: automatic registration

Possession of indecent photographs of children under 16 (1988 Criminal Justice Act, Section 160)

Where the offender is under 18: 12 months' imprisonment

Where the offender is 18 or above: automatic registration

Rape (1),[2] Assault by penetration (2)

Automatic registration

Sexual assault (3)

Where the offender is under 18: 12 months' imprisonment

Where the offender is 18 or above, and at least one of the following applies:

- the victim was under 18;
- the offender received a prison sentence;
- was detained in a hospital;
- was made the subject of a 12-month community sentence.

Causing sexual activity without consent (4) Rape of a child under 13 (5) Assault of a child under 13 by penetration (6)

Automatic registration

Sexual assault of a child under 13 (7)

Where the offender is under 18: 12 months' imprisonment

Where the offender is 18 or above: automatic registration

Causing or inciting a child under 13 to engage in sexual activity (8) Child sex offences committed by adults (9-12)

Automatic registration

Child sex offences committed by children or young persons (13)

(The offender will always be under 18): 12 months' imprisonment

Arranging or facilitating the commission of a child sex offence (14)

Where the offender is under 18: 12 months' imprisonment

Where the offender is 18 or above: automatic registration

Meeting a child following sexual grooming (15)

Automatic registration

Abuse of a position of trust (16-19)

Where the offender fulfils any of the following:

- received a prison sentence;
- was detained in a hospital;
- was made the subject of a 12-month community sentence.

Familial child sex offences (25-26)

Where the offender is under 18: 12 months' imprisonment

Where the offender is 18 or above: automatic registration

Offences against persons with a mental disorder (30-37)

Automatic registration

Care worker offences (38-41)

Where the offender is under 18: 12 months' imprisonment

Where the offender is 18 or above, and at least one of the following applies:

* received a prison sentence;
* was detained in a hospital
* was made the subject of a 12-month community sentence.

Paying for the sexual services of a child (47)

Where the victim was under 16:

And the offender was under 18: 12 months' imprisonment

And the offender was 18 or above: automatic registration

Administering a substance with intent (61)

Automatic registration

Committing an offence (62), or trespassing (63), with intent to commit a sexual offence

Where the offender is under 18: 12 months' imprisonment

Where the offender is 18 or above, and at least one of the following applies:

* the victim was under 18;
* received a prison sentence;
* was detained in a hospital;
* was made the subject of a 12-month community sentence.

Sex with an adult relative (64-65)

Where the offender is under 18: 12 months' imprisonment

Where the offender is 18 or above and where either of the following applies:

- received a prison sentence;
- was detained in a hospital.

Exposure (66)

Where the offender is under 18: 12 months' imprisonment

Where the offender is 18 or above, and at least one of the following applies:

- the victim was under 18;
- received a prison sentence;
- was detained in a hospital;
- was made the subject of a 12-month community sentence.

Voyeurism (67)

Where the offender is under 18: 12 months' imprisonment

Where the offender is 18 or above, and at least one of the following applies:

- the victim was under 18;
- received a prison sentence;
- was detained in a hospital;
- was made the subject of a 12-month community sentence.

Intercourse with an animal (69) or sexual penetration of a corpse (70)

Where the offender is under 18: 12 months' imprisonment

Where the offender is 18 or above, and at least one of the following applies:

- received a prison sentence;
- was detained in a hospital.

Relevant violent and other sexual offences (MAPPA category 2)

These offences are set out in schedule 15 of the 2003 Criminal Justice Act. An individual becomes a MAPPA category 2 case if he or she commits one of the following offences and receives a custodial sentence of 12 months or more. An individual will also be eligible for MAPPA (category 2) if: 'he [or she] is convicted by a court in England or Wales of murder' (2003 Criminal Justice Act, s.327(3)(a)).

1   Manslaughter.
2   Kidnapping.
3   False imprisonment.
4   An offence under Section 4 of the 1861 Offences Against the Person Act (c.100) (soliciting murder).
5   An offence under Section 16 of that Act (making threats to kill).
6   An offence under Section 18 of that Act (wounding with intent to cause grievous bodily harm).
7   An offence under Section 20 of that Act (malicious wounding).
8   An offence under Section 21 of that Act (attempting to choke, suffocate or strangle in order to commit or assist in committing an indictable offence).
9   An offence under Section 22 of that Act (using chloroform etc to commit or assist in the committing of any indictable offence).
10   An offence under Section 23 of that Act (maliciously administering poison, etc, so as to endanger life or inflict grievous bodily harm).
11   An offence under Section 27 of that Act (abandoning children).
12   An offence under Section 28 of that Act (causing bodily injury by explosives).
13   An offence under Section 29 of that Act (using explosives etc with intent to do grievous bodily harm).
14   An offence under Section 30 of that Act (placing explosives with intent to do bodily injury).
15   An offence under Section 31 of that Act (setting spring guns etc with intent to do grievous bodily harm).
16   An offence under Section 32 of that Act (endangering the safety of railway passengers).
17   An offence under Section 35 of that Act (injuring persons by furious driving).
18   An offence under Section 37 of that Act (assaulting officer preserving a wreck).
19   An offence under Section 38 of that Act (assault with intent to resist arrest).
20   An offence under Section 47 of that Act (assault occasioning actual bodily harm).
21   An offence under Section 2 of the 1883 Explosive Substances Act (c.3) (causing explosion likely to endanger life or property).
22   An offence under Section 3 of that Act (attempt to cause explosion, or making or keeping explosive with intent to endanger life or property).

23   An offence under Section 1 of the 1929 Infant Life (Preservation) Act (c.34) (child destruction).

24   An offence under Section 1 of the 1933 Children and Young Persons Act (c.12) (cruelty to children).

25   An offence under Section 1 of the 1938 Infanticide Act (c.36) (infanticide).

26   An offence under Section 16 of the 1968 Firearms Act (c.27) (possession of firearm with intent to endanger life).

27   An offence under Section 16A of that Act (possession of firearm with intent to cause fear of violence).

28   An offence under Section 17(1) of that Act (use of firearm to resist arrest).

29   An offence under Section 17(2) of that Act (possession of firearm at time of committing or being arrested for offence specified in Schedule 1 to that Act).

30   An offence under Section 18 of that Act (carrying a firearm with criminal intent).

31   An offence under Section 8 of the 1968 Theft Act (c.60) (robbery or assault with intent to rob).

32   An offence under Section 9 of that Act of burglary with intent to:
a. inflict grievous bodily harm on a person; or
b. do unlawful damage to a building or anything in it.

33   An offence under Section 10 of that Act (aggravated burglary).

34   An offence under Section 12A of that Act (aggravated vehicle-taking) involving an accident that caused the death of any person.

35   An offence of arson under Section 1 of the 1971 Criminal Damage Act (c.48).

36   An offence under Section 1(2) of that Act (destroying or damaging property) other than an offence of arson.

37   An offence under Section 1 of the 1982 Taking of Hostages Act (c.28) (hostage-taking).

38   An offence under Section 1 of the 1982 Aviation Security Act (c.36) (hijacking).

39   An offence under Section 2 of that Act (destroying, damaging or endangering the safety of aircraft).

40   An offence under Section 3 of that Act (other acts endangering or likely to endanger the safety of aircraft).

41   An offence under Section 4 of that Act (offences in relation to certain dangerous articles).

42   An offence under Section 127 of the 1983 Mental Health Act (c.20) (ill-treatment of patients).

43   An offence under Section 1 of the 1985 Prohibition of Female Circumcision Act (c.38) (prohibition of female circumcision).

44   An offence under Section 1 of the 1986 Public Order Act (c.64) (riot).

45   An offence under Section 2 of that Act (violent disorder).

46   An offence under Section 3 of that Act (affray).

47   An offence under Section 134 of the 1988 Criminal Justice Act (c.33) (torture).

48   An offence under Section 1 of the 1988 Road Traffic Act (c.52) (causing death by dangerous driving).

49   An offence under Section 3a of that Act (causing death by careless driving when under the influence of drink or drugs).

50   An offence under Section 1 of the 1990 Aviation and Maritime Security Act (c.31) (endangering safety at aerodromes).

51   An offence under Section 9 of that Act (hijacking of ships).

52   An offence under Section 10 of that Act (seizing or exercising control of fixed platforms).

53   An offence under Section 11 of that Act (destroying fixed platforms or endangering their safety).

54   An offence under Section 12 of that Act (other acts endangering or likely to endanger safe navigation).

55   An offence under Section 13 of that Act (offences involving threats).

56   An offence under Part II of the 1994 Channel Tunnel (Security) Order (S.I 1994/570) (offences relating to Channel Tunnel trains and the tunnel system).

57   An offence under Section 4 of the 1997 Protection from Harassment Act (c.40) (putting people in fear of violence).

58   An offence under Section 29 of the 1998 Crime and Disorder Act (c.37) (racially or religiously aggravated assaults).

59   An offence falling within Section 31(1)(a) or (b) of that Act (racially or religiously aggravated offences under Section 4 or 4a of the 1986 Public Order Act (c.64).

60   An offence under Section 51 or 52 of the 2001 International Criminal Court Act (c.17) (genocide, crimes against humanity, war crimes and related offences), other than one involving murder.

61   An offence under Section 1 of the 2003 Female Genital Mutilation Act (c.31) (female genital mutilation).

62   An offence under Section 2 of that Act (assisting a girl to mutilate her own genitalia).

63   An offence under Section 3 of that Act (assisting a non-UK person to mutilate overseas a girl's genitalia).

64   An offence of:
       a. aiding, abetting, counselling, procuring or inciting the commission of an offence specified in this part of this schedule;
       b. conspiring to commit an offence so specified; or
       c. attempting to commit an offence so specified.

65   An attempt to commit murder or a conspiracy to commit murder.

Specified sexual offences

66   An offence under Section 1 of the 1956 Sexual Offences Act (c.69) (rape).

67   An offence under Section 2 of that Act (procurement of a woman by threats).

68   An offence under Section 3 of that Act (procurement of a woman by false pretences).
69   An offence under Section 4 of that Act (administering drugs to obtain or facilitate intercourse).
70   An offence under Section 5 of that Act (intercourse with a girl under 13).
71   An offence under Section 6 of that Act (intercourse with a girl under 16).
72   An offence under Section 7 of that Act (intercourse with a defective).
73   An offence under Section 9 of that Act (procurement of a defective).
74   An offence under Section 10 of that Act (incest by a man).
75   An offence under Section 11 of that Act (incest by a woman).
76   An offence under Section 14 of that Act (indecent assault on a woman).
77   An offence under Section 15 of that Act (indecent assault on a man).
78   An offence under Section 16 of that Act (assault with intent to commit buggery).
79   An offence under Section 17 of that Act (abduction of a woman by force or for the sake of her property).
80   An offence under Section 19 of that Act (abduction of an unmarried girl under 18 from parent or guardian).
81   An offence under Section 20 of that Act (abduction of an unmarried girl under 16 from parent or guardian).
82   An offence under Section 21 of that Act (abduction of a defective from parent or guardian).
83   An offence under Section 22 of that Act (causing prostitution of women).
84   An offence under Section 23 of that Act (procuration of a girl under 21).
85   An offence under Section 24 of that Act (detention of a woman in a brothel).
86   An offence under Section 25 of that Act (permitting a girl under 13 to use premises for intercourse).
87   An offence under Section 26 of that Act (permitting a girl under 16 to use premises for intercourse).
88   An offence under Section 27 of that Act (permitting a defective to use premises for intercourse).
89   An offence under Section 28 of that Act (causing or encouraging the prostitution of, intercourse with or indecent assault on a girl under 16).
90   An offence under Section 29 of that Act (causing or encouraging the prostitution of a defective).
91   An offence under Section 32 of that Act (soliciting by men).
92   An offence under Section 33 of that Act (keeping a brothel).
93   An offence under Section 128 of the 1959 Mental Health Act (c.72) (sexual intercourse with patients).
94   An offence under Section 1 of the 1960 Indecency with Children Act (c.33) (indecent conduct towards a young child).
95   An offence under Section 4 of the 1967 Sexual Offences Act (c.60) (procuring others to commit homosexual acts).
96   An offence under Section 5 of that Act (living on earnings of male prostitution).

97   An offence under Section 9 of the 1968 Theft Act (c.60) (burglary with intent to commit rape).

98   An offence under Section 54 of the 1977 Criminal Law Act (c.45) (inciting girl under 16 to have incestuous sexual intercourse).

99   An offence under Section 1 of the 1978 Protection of Children Act (c.37) (indecent photographs of children).

100   An offence under Section 170 of the 1979 Customs and Excise Management Act (c.2) (penalty for fraudulent evasion of duty, etc) in relation to goods prohibited to be imported under Section 42 of the 1876 Customs Consolidation Act (c.36) (indecent or obscene articles).

101   An offence under Section 160 of the 1988 Criminal Justice Act (c.33) (possession of an indecent photograph of a child).

102   An offence under Section 1 of the 2003 Sexual Offences Act (c.42) (rape).

103   An offence under Section 2 of that Act (assault by penetration).

104   An offence under Section 3 of that Act (sexual assault).

105   An offence under Section 4 of that Act (causing a person to engage in sexual activity without consent).

106   An offence under Section 5 of that Act (rape of a child under 13).

107   An offence under Section 6 of that Act (assault of a child under 13 by penetration).

108   An offence under Section 7 of that Act (sexual assault of a child under 13).

109   An offence under Section 8 of that Act (causing or inciting a child under 13 to engage in sexual activity).

110   An offence under Section 9 of that Act (sexual activity with a child).

111   An offence under Section 10 of that Act (causing or inciting a child to engage in sexual activity).

112   An offence under Section 11 of that Act (engaging in sexual activity in the presence of a child).

113   An offence under Section 12 of that Act (causing a child to watch a sexual act).

114   An offence under Section 13 of that Act (child sex offences committed by children or young persons).

115   An offence under Section 14 of that Act (arranging or facilitating commission of a child sex offence).

116   An offence under Section 15 of that Act (meeting a child following sexual grooming, etc).

117   An offence under Section 16 of that Act (abuse of a position of trust: sexual activity with a child).

118   An offence under Section 17 of that Act (abuse of a position of trust: causing or inciting a child to engage in sexual activity).

119   An offence under Section 18 of that Act (abuse of a position of trust: sexual activity in the presence of a child).

120   An offence under Section 19 of that Act (abuse of a position of trust: causing a child to watch a sexual act).

121   An offence under Section 25 of that Act (sexual activity with a child family member).

122   An offence under Section 26 of that Act (inciting a child family member to engage in sexual activity).

123   An offence under Section 30 of that Act (sexual activity with a person with a mental disorder impeding choice).

124   An offence under Section 31 of that Act (causing or inciting a person with a mental disorder impeding choice to engage in sexual activity).

125   An offence under Section 32 of that Act (engaging in sexual activity in the presence of a person with a mental disorder impeding choice).

126   An offence under Section 33 of that Act (causing a person with a mental disorder impeding choice to watch a sexual act).

127   An offence under Section 34 of that Act (inducement, threat or deception to procure sexual activity with a person with a mental disorder).

128   An offence under Section 35 of that Act (causing a person with a mental disorder to engage in or agree to engage in sexual activity by inducement, threat or deception).

129   An offence under Section 36 of that Act (engaging in sexual activity in the presence, procured by inducement, threat or deception, of a person with a mental disorder).

130   An offence under Section 37 of that Act (causing a person with a mental disorder to watch a sexual act by inducement, threat or deception).

131   An offence under Section 38 of that Act (care workers: sexual activity with a person with a mental disorder).

132   An offence under Section 39 of that Act (care workers: causing or inciting sexual activity).

133   An offence under Section 40 of that Act (care workers: sexual activity in the presence of a person with a mental disorder).

134   An offence under Section 41 of that Act (care workers: causing a person with a mental disorder to watch a sexual act).

135   An offence under Section 47 of that Act (paying for the sexual services of a child).

136   An offence under Section 48 of that Act (causing or inciting child prostitution or pornography).

137   An offence under Section 49 of that Act (controlling a child prostitute or a child involved in pornography).

138   An offence under Section 50 of that Act (arranging or facilitating child prostitution or pornography).

139   An offence under Section 52 of that Act (causing or inciting prostitution for gain).

140   An offence under Section 53 of that Act (controlling prostitution for gain).

141   An offence under Section 57 of that Act (trafficking into the UK for sexual exploitation).

142   An offence under Section 58 of that Act (trafficking within the UK for sexual exploitation).

143 An offence under Section 59 of that Act (trafficking out of the UK for sexual exploitation).

144 An offence under Section 61 of that Act (administering a substance with intent).

145 An offence under Section 62 of that Act (committing an offence with intent to commit a sexual offence).

146 An offence under Section 63 of that Act (trespass with intent to commit a sexual offence).

147 An offence under Section 64 of that Act (sex with an adult relative: penetration).

148 An offence under Section 65 of that Act (sex with an adult relative: consenting to penetration).

149 An offence under Section 66 of that Act (exposure).

150 An offence under Section 67 of that Act (voyeurism).

151 An offence under Section 69 of that Act (intercourse with an animal).

152 An offence under Section 70 of that Act (sexual penetration of a corpse).

153 An offence of:
   a. aiding, abetting, counselling, procuring or inciting the commission of an offence specified in this part of this schedule;
   b. conspiring to commit an offence so specified;
   c. attempting to commit an offence so specified.

Notes

[1] As set out in the 2003 Criminal Justice Act s.325-7.

[2] The numbers in brackets here denote the section number in the 2003 Sexual Offences Act.